CONFLICTS *in* CONSCIOUSNESS

CONFLICTS
in CONSCIOUSNESS

T. S. Eliot's Poetry and Criticism

DAVID SPURR

University of Illinois Press
URBANA CHICAGO LONDON

This book is printed on acid-free paper.

Publication of this work was supported in part by a grant
from the Andrew W. Mellon Foundation.

Library of Congress Cataloging in Publication Data

Spurr, David, 1949–
  Conflicts in consciousness.

  Bibliography: p.
  Includes index.
  1. Eliot, T. S. (Thomas Stearns), 1888–1965—
Criticism and interpretation. I. Title.
PS3509.L43Z8696   1983   821'.912   82-17491
ISBN 0-252-01026-4

Grateful acknowledgment is made to the following for permission
to quote copyrighted materials:

Faber and Faber Ltd., for extracts from the *Collected Poems 1909–
1962* by T. S. Eliot, including *The Waste Land, Ash-Wednesday,
Four Quartets,* and other short poems; copyright 1936, 1963.

Harcourt Brace Jovanovich, Inc., for excerpts from the *Collected
Poems 1909–1962* by T. S. Eliot, including "Burnt Norton," "East
Coker," "The Dry Salvages," and "Little Gidding" in *Four Quar-
tets,* and *The Cocktail Party*; copyright 1936 by Harcourt Brace
Jovanovich, Inc.; copyright © 1943, 1950, 1963, 1964 by T. S.
Eliot; copyright 1971, 1978 by Esme Valerie Eliot.

Yeats Eliot Review, for permission to reprint the article "Conflicts
of Mind and Vision in 'Prufrock' and 'Gerontion,'" 6 (1980):
10–15.

Wayne State University Press, for permission to reprint "T. S.
Eliot's Divided Critical Sensibility," *Criticism* 23 (1981): 58–76.

FOR
Catherine Millar Spurr

Contents

Acknowledgments

I AM INDEBTED to Professor George Bornstein for his thorough criticism and generous encouragement at every stage of this work. I also thank Professor Ross Chambers, who read the manuscript with care and provided invaluable advice.

The Horace H. Rackham School of Graduate Studies, University of Michigan, provided a grant in support of this work.

Introduction

I N HIS 1930 ESSAY on Baudelaire, T. S. Eliot suggests that the
formal concerns of some nineteenth-century poets support or
conceal "an inner disorder" and that in Baudelaire's poems "the
content of feeling is constantly bursting the receptacle."[1] Eliot's
distinctions between form and content, and between conflicting
elements of the Romantic sensibility, may or may not further our
understanding of Baudelaire and his contemporaries; they do,
however, both suggest and sanction a valuable line of approach to
his own poetry. A forty-year tradition of Eliot scholarship has
established plausible grounds for narrative coherence in each of
Eliot's major poems, and continues to reveal an ever-widening
range of literary influences on the poet's work. This same tradition, however, has left largely unexplored the sources of structural tension in Eliot's poems and the problem of relating these
tensions to a developing poetic consciousness. Eliot himself says
of Baudelaire's poems, "Their excellence of form, their perfection
of phrasing, and their superficial coherence, may give them the
appearance of presenting a definite and final state of mind."[2] But
then he goes on to argue a discrepancy between what he calls
their external and internal forms. In a similar paradox, Eliot
scholarship has created a superficial coherence in his work by
assuming a definite state of mind or point of view in each poem.
In their tendency to accept Eliot's critical and poetic statements
at face value, scholars have overlooked the fundamental conflicts
that lie below the surface of Eliot's language.

While the mainstream of this critical tradition continues to
take Eliot's pronouncements on poetry as the authoritative guide

to his own work, the influence of emerging critical methodologies in recent years has generated a subversive countercurrent to this tradition. This relatively new critical attitude attempts to identify the submerged conflicts of Eliot's language and generally sees his poetry, like his critical writings and even his personality, as divided against itself in various ways. The contributions of critics like C. K. Stead, Bernard Bergonzi, and George Bornstein[3] create at least two favorable conditions for a systematic study of Eliot's consciousness in all its complexity: first, they point to an essential polarity in Eliot's work that can be identified with both formal and thematic elements in his poems; and, second, they free the critic from traditional explanations of a poem based on searches for narrative sequence, allegorical meaning, or literary allusion, and allow him to focus on the nature of poetic language as arising directly from the poet's own "obscure creative impulse."[4] Even if the unconscious motivation of such language can never be known in the historical or biographical sense, its hypothetical nature can enrich our experience of the text by allowing us to see the poem as a stage or field for the enactment of conflicts whose origins lie in the poet's mind.

The reading of Eliot that I am proposing, then, shares with psychoanalytic approaches to literature the attempt to establish connections between the text and the author's unconscious, while it also follows certain deconstructive procedures in its refusal to take for granted the textual coherence of any poem. This kind of reading not only treats the poem as reflecting the inner forces of the poet's imagination; it also assumes that these forces may run at cross-purposes to one another; the multilayered quality of psychological motivation accounts for a similar quality of the text.

Those who have identified the problem of a divided sensibility in Eliot's poetry all make a basic distinction between forces of order and disorder. My own study leads to a somewhat different formulation, which sees Eliot's poems as enacting a dramatic rivalry between the two kinds of order, one rational and a product of the poet's intellectual power, the other intuitive and a product of the more primitive and spontaneous aspect of the poet's imagination.

Intellectual order, or the poet's attempt to make rational sense out of the world around him, manifests itself typically in Eliot's images of concentration, division, and apportionment. The impulse "to have squeezed the universe into a ball," as well as the image of a "still point of the turning world," reflects a desire to master existence through the phenomenon of spatial concentration. A voice cries out of *The Waste Land*, "Shall I at least set my lands in order?" while a later voice can state with confidence in divine dispensation: "This is the land. We have our inheritance." The aspect of the poet's sensibility that seeks a rationally comprehensible world often seeks the intervention of forces from outside this world as external sources of order. The prophet Lazarus, Christ the tiger, the speaking thunder, and the Lady of silences all represent other-worldly forces to which the poet looks, however momentarily or equivocally, for a way of defining his own world. The function of such imagery is continually supported on another level by the language of mental activity—of thought, knowledge, and memory—which reveals the poet's preoccupation with the nature of the conscious mind and its relation to experience:

> ... but the sudden illumination—
> We had the experience but missed the meaning,
> And approach to the meaning restores the experience
> In a different form, beyond any meaning
> We can assign to happiness.
>
> (*The Dry Salvages*, 92–96)

These approaches to the meaning or "acts of mind" embodied in Eliot's language and imagery have in common a tendency to *impose* order on a world that, left to itself, would fly apart at the seams or drift forever in aimlessness: "We cannot think of a time that is oceanless / Or of an ocean not littered with wastage." The ordering principle thus appears as external to a world in need of order; Lazarus must come from the dead, the thunder must speak from above, the mind must deliberately "construct something / Upon which to rejoice."

"There is a logic of the imagination as well as a logic of concepts," Eliot writes in the preface to his translation of Saint-John Perse's *Anabase*.[5] Lifting this remark out of its original context, we may borrow Eliot's distinction between imagination and conceptual thinking in order to define the polarity of his own poetic consciousness. Over against his "diurnal" tendency to master experience through images of division and concentration and through a corresponding vocabulary of conscious mental activity, there lies a "nocturnal" aspect of the poet that seeks to describe a set of relations which could not be defined in terms of a purely conceptual framework—Eliot's relatively undeveloped version of Baudelaire's "ténébreuse et profonde unité." By referring casually to this diurnal tendency as "intellect" and to the opposing nocturnal tendency as "imagination," we may say that where the intellect seeks control of subject over object, the imagination joins the two: "You are the music while the music lasts." The ordering principle of the material of the imagination arises internally rather than being imposed from without, as in the figure of the Chinese jar, which "Moves perpetually in its stillness." As the imagination conceives of order dynamically rather than statically, so "the detail of the pattern is movement."

Ordinarily when we speak of poetic imagination we use this term in a general way to include the various psychological phenomena that enter into the creative act. Certainly in this conventional sense all poetic images—natural or supernatural, architectural or mechanical—are expressive of the imagination. But for purely practical purposes here I wish to limit the meaning of *imagination* by using it exclusively in connection with the isolated aspect of Eliot's consciousness that produces his version of the Romantic or Symbolist vision, often dreamlike in quality, which conforms to organic rather than conceptual principles of order. This "visionary" imagination creates in Eliot's poetry a symbolic structure that defines itself primarily in images of flight, expansion, depth, and response. The spatial character of these images combines with their semantic value to create a set of interlocking themes that together constitute Eliot's Romantic-Symbolist vision: purity, the descent to a submerged inner world, the merging of the human and the natural. This kind of approach will allow us to compare Prufrock's underwater sojourns with, say, the death of the Phoenecian sailor in *The Waste Land*, and eventually to ascribe these scenes to a common sphere of the poet's imagination.[6]

The forces of imagination moving through images of the kind I have just described constantly challenge the intellect for domination of the poet's sensibility in a way that affects the overall structure of each poem. The poet's intellect serves his will; but as Stead remarks, Eliot relies for inspiration on creative moments that occur independently of the will. Both kinds of order are positive, but they remain for the most part unreconciled: the imagination in its subaqueous plunges and its angelic flights tends to evade the task of conquering experience that the intellect sets for itself, while the intellect in turn denies the validity of the imagination's life, of "The empty forms between the ivory gates."

Between the ideals of imaginative order and intellectual order in Eliot's poetry lies a disordered middle ground, a "place of disaffection" where the poet records mimetically the raw data of seemingly random experience, without according it any particular ontological value: "empty bottles, sandwich papers, / Silk handkerchiefs, cardboard boxes, cigarette ends." This area of the poet's sensibility belongs neither to the intellect nor to the imagination in the limited way we have used these terms as principles of order; disorder is simply disorder. The poetic persona remains for a time passive in the face of his chaotic universe. This is, of course, to treat the disorder of experience as part of the poem's subject matter, the monster of horror and *ennui* the poet-hero must either conquer or evade. Thus in Eliot's work the images of disorder have their own structures of fragmentation, isolation, circular movement, endless repetition, aimless wandering, and random profusion:

> Tumid apathy with no concentration
> Men and bits of paper, whirled by the cold wind
> That blows before and after time,
> Wind in and out of unwholesome lungs
> Time before and time after.
>
> (*Burnt Norton*, 103–7)

Time here is the dragon of endless succession, which if the poet cannot slay ("Only through time time is conquered"), he can flee from at privileged moments into the timeless sanctuaries of a visionary world populated by mermaids, hyacinth girls, laughing children, and antic musicians.

The present study of these movements in Eliot's work concentrates on what have been regarded traditionally as his major poems; they also happen to be his longer poems and, therefore, have sufficient scope and magnitude to allow the full development of conflicts in the poet's mind. While recent critical work on the problem of Eliot's divided sensibility has concentrated on the early poems, my own research focuses more closely on the later half of his poetic career. More important, this study seeks not simply to identify the underlying oppositions in each successive poem, but also to establish a general scheme of Eliot's career whereby the changing nature of these structures may be observed through time.

One could describe this career as a series of confrontations with a visionary imagination that Eliot can neither conquer nor reconcile wholly with other aspects of his poetic consciousness. The nature of these confrontations changes with the evolution of Eliot's poetic identity as reflected in the character of the "speaker" in each poem. The rivalry between intellectual and imaginative order establishes itself in the two great poems of Eliot's early period, *The Love Song of J. Alfred Prufrock* (published 1917) and *Gerontion* (published 1920). In each of these poems the failure of a self-conscious mind to master its own situation amid images of random profusion and labyrinthine space leads to escape into images of purity, flight, and intimacy. The form of the dramatic monologue, however, provides an ironic distance that allows Eliot to discredit his visionary imagination. *Prufrock* takes a dream-vision worthy of Nerval or Baudelaire and attaches it to a Laforguian character "Full of high sentence, but a bit obtuse." The speaker of *Gerontion* dismisses the Mallarméan flight of his imagination ("Gull against the wind") as "Thoughts of a dry brain in a dry season." In both cases the visionary imagery testifies to a source of inspiration that runs at cross-purposes to the poem's surface rhetoric.

Eliot's poetic persona breaks down in *The Waste Land* (published 1922) to produce a multiplicity of voices scattered throughout the poem. This phenomenon combined with the actual fragmentation of linguistic forms sabotages the visionary imagination by allowing it to surface only in bits and pieces uttered by a profusion of different speakers. One hears at different points in the poem and in apparently unrelated contexts a Wagnerian sailor singing from the mast, Verlaine's children singing in the tower, and a hermit-thrush singing in the pine trees. On one level of reading, the isolated nature of such fragments simply conforms to the poem's general ethos of disorder and random destruction. On another level, however, the images conform to a symbolic structure that joins images of elevation, music, and purity to images of descent and fusion with nature. This symbolic alliance points to a visionary inner world of the poet's consciousness that remains intact despite the poem's more obvious rhetoric of collapse, like oceanic depths undisturbed by storms at the surface.

The disintegration of Eliot's persona in *The Waste Land* signals a crisis of poetic identity, which, after a long period of silence, leaves him with the notion of speaker as mask alone in *The Hollow Men* (published 1925): "Such deliberate disguises / Rat's coat, crowskin, crossed staves." This denial of identity provides Eliot with a new line of assault on the visionary imagination. If the speaker amounts only to a scarecrow's mask, his Edenic vision can only belong to "Death's dream kingdom." This very abdication of self-identity prepares for the adoption of a Christian persona in *Ash-Wednesday* (published 1930); for in Eliot's version of the ascetic process, the individual must purge himself of his own being in order to be filled by God. In this poem Eliot's Romantic vision surfaces in images of expansion and correspondence with nature that repeatedly frustrate more conscious movements of concentration and *askesis*—the Christian process of self-purgation involving the deliberate "emptying-out" of the soul. The speaker's Christian role allows him to attack the natural vision on theological grounds: the attraction to nature distracts the soul from God.

Eliot's role as the aging poet in *Four Quartets* (published 1943) signals a final attempt to reconcile the divergent forces of his sensibility by assimilating the forces of the imagination to a larger conceptual framework involving notions of time. Having evolved beyond an orthodox Christian attitude, Eliot now comes closer than ever to his Romantic and Symbolist predecessors by ascribing mystical significance to his moments of vision. Imagination once more conflicts with intellect, as the poet attempts unsuccessfully to formulate a worldly meaning for his mystical vision. The poet's "undisciplined squads of emotion" again defy the intellectual order which the poet attempts to impose on his experience when they move toward a form of order independent of the intellect. The struggle to conquer time cannot succeed when what the poet really values is not to be found in time.

In certain respects the fundamental divisions of Eliot's consciousness can be seen as paradigmatic for the poetic act itself: to some extent all poets are drawn to both rational and visionary unities in giving form to an essentially chaotic experience. But what sets Eliot apart from his great spiritual and artistic models— Dante, Baudelaire, Yeats—is the intensity with which this polar opposition pulls the text apart at various levels and therefore becomes itself a kind of demon to be exorcised. It may be said of the other great poets, I believe, that a rational construct provides, trellislike, the very framework that allows the visionary experience to unfold: Dante's ordered ascent, Baudelaire's controlled sonnet form, Yeats's dialectic between self and image. Eliot's visionary unities, on the other hand, surface around the edges or between the crevices of his rational construct. While other poets have brought about the fusion of intellect and imagination, in Eliot these forces either diverge or come together in recurrent struggles for supremacy.

The terms in which I have described the evolution of Eliot's embattled sensibility make it possible to divide his career into two stages. In the first stage, the ironic persona of the early poems eventually disintegrates under the pressure of the poet's inner conflicts; *The Waste Land* shows us a fragmented persona whose different voices express opposing factions of the poet's consciousness. The process that culminates in *The Waste Land* has its parallels with the process that begins with *The Hollow Men* and culminates in the *Four Quartets*.

In the second stage of Eliot's poetic evolution, he adopts an external set of values rather than an ironic persona, but this new role serves somewhat the same function by providing a structure to combat the forces of a visionary imagination. In this respect Eliot's Gerontion and Eliot's converted Christian unite in a common defense against an imagination that threatens to engulf the poet's mind—hence, in *Ash-Wednesday*, the simultaneous love and fear of "the lost lilac and the lost sea voices" and the speaker's redoubled effort at concentration and prayer: "Teach us to care and not to care / Teach us to sit still." The *Four Quartets* represent a development beyond the limited context of this Christian poem, just as *The Waste Land* signaled a development beyond the dramatic monologue and the quatrain poem. Rather than a final synthesis of psychological values, however, Eliot's last great work enacts an elaborate unfolding of divergent impulses that it can only claim to unite on a rhetorical level. For all their deliberate formal order, the *Four Quartets* reveal as much internal divisiveness as does *The Waste Land*.

A final chapter of the present work shows how this evolution of Eliot's sensibility develops in his critical writings as well as in his poems. The tensions involved here lend strength to poetry, but apparently they can be ruinous to the poet himself. Either from the ascetic demands of spiritual devotion or from weariness with continual raids on the inarticulate, Eliot allows the *Four Quartets* to stand as his farewell to poetry. From this point on, his critical work also loses much of its bite, taking the form of official pronouncements from the elder statesman of letters: "What Is a Classic?", "The Aims of Education," "The Classics and the Man of Letters."

An analysis of Eliot's work that divides his sensibility into separate and identifiable components no doubt threatens to become a reductivist portrayal of an extremely complex artistic mind and, in a way, imitates Eliot's own passion for logic and apportionment. The violence of such an approach may perhaps be tolerated, but with the reminder that the notion of "forces" and "movements" in the poet's consciousness are intended simply as metaphors for various levels of the text. Only in the interest of elucidating the text is it useful to speak, again metaphorically, of its sources in "sensibility," "mind," "intellect," or "imagination." Finally, an analysis of a poet's work that discovers unresolved conflicts and ambiguities should not necessarily be regarded as an attack. On the contrary, it seems more likely that the life of an artist's work is sustained by the energy of inner forces in opposition, whether one calls them intellect and imagination, conscious and unconscious, or thought and emotion. Eliot's poetry represents a consciousness whose emotional intensity derives from an awareness of its own inner divisions; its strength lies in its refusal to allow the controlling power of the intellect or the controlling form of the poem to annihilate the dark impulses of horror and ecstasy.

NOTES

1. T. S. Eliot, *Selected Essays* (New York: Harcourt, Brace & World, 1964), p. 375.
2. Ibid.
3. C. K. Stead, in *The New Poetic: Yeats to Eliot* (London: Hutchinson, 1964), described Eliot's poetic technique as an attempt to balance a rational, constructive will that "illegitimately persuades at the expense of complex truth," with a passive part of the mind that "negatively comprehends complexity, and provides images to embody it, but fails on its own to construct, assert, or even affirm" (p. 126). Bernard Bergonzi, in *T. S. Eliot* (New York: Collier, 1972), renewed Stead's inquiry into the divided nature of Eliot's sensibility by locating an underlying tension in the poems between the disorder of sexual desire and a conscious effort to establish order. George Bornstein, in *Transformations of Romanticism in Yeats, Eliot, and Stevens* (Chicago: University of Chicago Press, 1976), argued that Eliot's anti-Romanticism resulted from a fear of his own imagination as it opened on a terrifying unconscious; Eliot's work thus became a struggle to control the forces of that imagination through various textual strategies.
4. Bergonzi, *T. S. Eliot*, p. 92.
5. T. S. Eliot, trans., *Anabasis: A Poem by Saint-John Perse* (London: Faber & Faber, 1959), p. 10.
6. Michel Benamou, in *Wallace Stevens and the Symbolist Imagination* (Princeton: Princeton University Press, 1972), provides a precedent for this approach. Benamou demonstrates that the theories of philosophers such as Gaston Bachelard and Gilbert Durand can establish links between unconscious psychological values and forms of poetic expression, especially imagery.

CONFLICTS *in* CONSCIOUSNESS

CHAPTER ONE

Psychic Battles in Prufrock and Gerontion

AT A POINT late enough in his career for him to reflect objectively on the nature of his own past achievements. T. S. Eliot offers a description of the creative process that portrays the poet as locked in battle with the forces of his own unconscious. Following a suggestion of the German poet Gottfried Benn, Eliot locates the beginnings of a poem in an "unknown, dark *psychic material*—we might say, the octopus or angel with which the poet struggles."[1] The poet must subdue these impulses by confining them within the proper form, even while the material itself, if it does not impose its own form, is likely to repeat "Not that! Not that!" in the face of each unsuccessful attempt at formal organization.

This notion of the poet as adversary to his own primary inspiration suggests a fundamental opposition in Eliot's work that has not been illuminated by critics who regard each poem as representing a coherent "point of view": "the deterioration of modern civilization," "the need for spiritual rebirth." While this opposition may become most intense at a point when Eliot's intellectual and religious beliefs are most firmly entrenched, it nonetheless arises early in his career to determine the structure of major poems such as *The Love Song of J. Alfred Prufrock* (written 1911) and *Gerontion* (written 1919). Despite their differences in style and tone, both of these poems give voice to a mind

---

Parts of this chapter were published in an article entitled "Psychic Conflict in *Prufrock* and *Gerontion*" in the *Yeats Eliot Review* 6 (1979) and are reprinted here by permission of the publisher.

struggling to impose order on the more intractable elements of its own nature. In each case the frustrations of the rage for intellectual order ultimately give way to the language of visionary experience with its own form of order, a product of the synthetic energy of the imagination rather than the conceptual power of the conscious intellect. The mind trades its battle with the octopus of disordered experience for the temptations of angelic vision.

The technique of the dramatic monologue provides the young Eliot with a means of enacting this psychic drama without first having established his own secure poetic identity. Robert Langbaum notes that in general the use of a speaker who can be named enables the poet to dramatize a situation "the possibilities of which he may want to explore"[2]; the poet by the same token avoids some of the problems associated with the notion of "self-expression." In *Prufrock* and *Gerontion* Eliot uses this device to contain the visionary flights or plunges of his imagination; the poet theoretically can maintain a safe distance from his "dark psychic material" by interposing an ironic mask. The same device has allowed traditional Eliot scholars to ignore the presence of any Romantic or Symbolist vision in these poems; by taking Eliot purely at face value, they can interpret everything in the poem as simply the exposition of a dramatic character. For Elisabeth Schneider, Prufrock "knows love at a distance only, and with its back turned, for the mermaids, as he observes ruefully, are 'riding seaward.' "[3] This kind of approach assumes that we are able to separate clearly the author of *Prufrock* from the character of that name in the way that we separate Browning from his Bishop Blougram or Fra Lippo Lippi. But the very ambiguity of Eliot's dramatic technique makes it possible to read the poem directly in terms of the consciousness behind the ironic mask. Thus Hugh Kenner describes *Gerontion* as a "zone" of consciousness that amounts to "an auditory illusion within the confines of which the components of the poem circulate and co-exist."[4]

In terms of the actual language and imagery of *Prufrock* and *Gerontion*, these components appear in a way that allows us to distinguish three major kinds of mental activity: (1) the conscious desire for purposive movement and direction—"I have not made this show purposelessly"; (2) an antithetical tendency toward aimlessness—"In the room the women come and go";

and (3) the resultant impulse for flight, both in a literal sense and in the sense of *evasion*—"Gull against the wind." This three-sided war is waged on another level in terms of the mind's relation to the outside world or to a separate inner world of the self. The conscious desire for discourse ("Shall I say"), frustrated by isolation and the inarticulate ("It is impossible to say"), finally gives over to correspondence or sexual union, the nonconceptual awareness of forming a whole with other beings or elements ("We have lingered in the chambers of the sea"). At the risk of appearing overly schematic, one could organize these various structuring forces in the following manner:

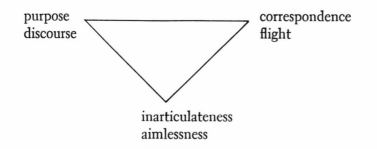

purpose · correspondence
discourse · flight

inarticulateness
aimlessness

In both poems the mental battle between purpose and aimlessness on one level and between discourse and the inarticulate on another builds gradually to a point where the informing consciousness flees into its own visionary world of purity.

The aspect of this analysis that attaches psychological values to image structure, as well as to more obvious linguistic forms, has its sources in the works of theorists such as Gaston Bachelard and Gilbert Durand, both of whom focus on the *spatial orientation* of imagery as an index to consciousness. In this case such an approach can expand on recent inquiries into the divided nature of Eliot's sensibility and provide a new methodological basis for tracing his poetic evolution. It increases the dimensions, for example, of the tension, noted by C. K. Stead, in *Prufrock* between an "editing consciousness" and an "unfulfilled sexual aspiration"; at the same time it widens the implications of George Bornstein's distinction between passages which yoke images together by association and those which acquire a developmental pattern according to laws of imagination.[5]

1

Prufrock establishes a dialectic between constructive intellect and disordered elements of consciousness that builds to a climax late in the poem, finally yielding to the flight into an inner world of visionary union. From the beginning, the speaker's repeated statements of purpose or destination are always countered by images of spatial disorder, meaningless repetition, fragmentation, isolation, and mental distraction. The sense of destination implied in the imperative "Let us go," for example, contrasts with the feeling of aimless wandering through labyrinthine time and space conveyed by images of "restless nights in one-night cheap hotels" and of "Streets that follow like a tedious argument." The sense of urgency conveyed by the final line of the initial verse-paragraph is immediately deflated by the lopsided couplet that describes the place of the "visit": "In the room the women come and go / Talking of Michelangelo." The purposive "And indeed there will be time" loses its rhetorical force in the parallel between the amorphous yellow smoke that "slides along the street" and that part of the mind which also roams the streets. The intention "To prepare a face to meet the faces that you meet" may sound like an assertion of the will, but the line mocks itself in inane repetition, and its suggestion of the dandy's mask only intensifies the sense of isolation expressed in the epigraph (*"di questo fondo non tornò vivo alcun"*) and in the image of "half-deserted streets."

This juxtaposition of purposive action and increased isolation is parodied fifteen lines later, where the theme of dandyism resurfaces. Here the collar mounts "firmly" to the chin and is "asserted" by a simple pin; but, of course, the clothing acts as one more barrier between the speaker and the world, while it fails to serve as protection: "(They will say: 'But how his arms and legs are thin!')."

The poem gradually begins to reveal a mind that, while it searches for order, simultaneously rebels against existing forms of order seen as inadequate to the mind's desire for meaning. The carefully tailored suit, the "works and days of hands," the "taking of toast and tea," even the notion of time itself, are all artificial constructs that the speaker, whether consciously or not, seeks to destroy: to "murder and create," to "Disturb the universe." The insistent if self-doubting references to daring and presumption come from a mind dimly aware of being trapped within the constraints of what Romantic poets have called the "calculating faculty."

The themes of aimlessness and isolation developed earlier in the poem now extend to forms of knowledge, measurement, and formulation. The knowledge of voices "Beneath the music from a farther room" only adds to a feeling of separation from the voices and music. Measurement reduces life to trivial repetition: "I have measured out my life with coffee spoons"; and the formulating power of language paralyzes the speaker in a position of helplessness: "when I am formulated, sprawling on a pin." The desire to "spit out all the butt-ends of my days and ways" recalls the "works and days" of thirty lines earlier and other images of waste and fragmentation symptomatic of disconnected experience: the "sawdust restaurants with oyster-shells."

If the formulating eyes do not frustrate the speaker's attempt to rid himself of all this detritus, then the sensual distraction of "Arms that are braceleted and white and bare" will. When he asks "Is it perfume from a dress / That makes me so digress?" the digression is from the kind of purposive action that could conceivably free him from the squirrel cage of his existence. These arms, which "lie along a table, or wrap about a shawl," imitate the movement of the fog that "slides along the street" and "curled . . . about the house." Such images represent the serpentine and intractable nature of a universe against which the mind struggles in its rage for order.

The conflict between purposive action and aimless movement coincides throughout the poem with a similar thematic opposition between discourse and the inarticulate. The labyrinthine streets of the poem's beginning "follow like a tedious argument." This phrase makes a comparison between spatial form and verbal expression that recurs frequently in Eliot's poems: the inadequacies of language become a metaphor for the mind's tedium or lack of direction. The language of discourse, like the language of spatial movement, leads deceptively toward what appears as a destination in the "overwhelming question" before shutting the door in our faces: "Oh, do not ask, 'What is it?' "

The theme of abortive discourse has already surfaced in the "muttering retreats" that recall the sputtering, muttering street lamp of *Rhapsody on a Windy Night* (*Collected Poems*, p. 16),[6] another poem of this period. Images of this nature perform a paradoxically dual function common in Symbolist poetry: on one hand, as part of the "thousand sordid images" which constitute his soul (*CP*, p. 14), they signify the speaker's own articulateness; but at the same time they stand apart from the speaker, testifying to his inability to converse with his own natural surroundings: "You had such a vision of the street / As the street hardly understands" (*CP*, p. 14).

Prufrock once again offers a parallel between discourse and movement in the image of the women "talking of Michelangelo." Despite the ennobling subject matter, we know that the talk strays meaninglessly, because the women "come and go" like the restless figures of the *Inferno* who inspire the poem's epigraph. The image of endless perambulation contained in a room conforms to the poem's general technique of erecting structures, often architectural, to contain or oppose formless and unstructured material. The evening can be "spread out" only against a sky that has the rigidity of a table. The speaker wandering through half-deserted streets is nonetheless confined by the boundaries of his urban labyrinth. The feline fog of the second verse-paragraph sustains the theme of distension introduced in line two, as it spreads into corners, rubs up against window-panes, slips by the terrace, and curls about the house. Again the structures of architectural elevation stand in opposition to the "soft" images of horizontal distension; but all of this amounts to more than atmospheric detail: it provides a picture of the speaker's mind, where the temptations of sleep and the "soft October night" undermine the impulse to "murder and create" in seeking an intelligible response to a disordered universe.

Formal elements of the poem parallel these thematic oppositions between purpose and aimlessness, discourse and the inarticulate. In the initial verse-paragraph, for example, the direct imperatives of the first and final lines form a grammatical frame around the more syntactically equivocal series of comparisons, appositions, and modifying clauses lying between them—a strategy of containment that conforms to the mental processes at work in the poem as a whole. The constant repetition of phrases like "There will be time" and "How should I presume?" forms a syntactical counterpart to the monotonous redundance of a life measured out with coffee spoons. The repeated but ambiguous use of the second person pronoun relates to the speaker's problem in drawing a dividing line between himself and his surroundings. Just as the streets and yellow smoke seem to represent parts of the speaker's mind as well as an exterior landscape, the "you" he addresses shares this same quality of being both a part and an object of his consciousness.[7] Even if the beginning of the poem suggests the presence of two separate interlocutors, the two tend to overlap later in the poem, as when the speaker faces the problem of preparing "a face to meet the faces that you meet." Both belong to the same mind; the Laforguian *dédoublement* effected by this rhetorical use of the pronoun points once more to the underlying divisions of the speaker's consciousness, and prepares for a later attempt at self-definition.

Eliot separates the first sixty-nine lines of *Prufrock* from the next five by a row of spaced periods. The typographical device announces a shift in the direction of mental action, as the verse-paragraph beginning with line seventy ("Shall I say") stages a tentative attack on the inarticulate followed by a hasty retreat into the nether regions of the imagination. For the twenty lines leading up to this point, the poem has developed in each verse-paragraph a pattern according to which a series of declarative statements end in a question. Here the pattern reverses itself, and a question begins the passage: "Shall I say, I have gone at dusk through narrow streets / And watched the smoke that rises from the pipes / Of lonely men in shirt-sleeves, leaning out of windows?" The question is partly an exercise in self-ridicule, but it also represents an attempt to define the experience of a psyche in a way that a "formulated phrase" cannot. The labyrinthine passage and the behavior of the smoke have by now become familiar to the reader.

The speaker obviously identifies with the lonely men (despite their shirt-sleeves), and perhaps sees their leaning out of windows as symbolic of his own desire for contact with the world. But the suggestion that he actually *say* this to someone, that he might put it into words, presumes too much. The mind, once having ascended the stair to confront the world, now flees in the other direction, downward and inward to a primitive world of silence where forms of knowledge and discourse simply do not pertain: "I should have been a pair of ragged claws / Scuttling across the floors of silent seas." Kenner remarks, "not even the full crab, just the claws and the scuttle."[8] The words strip the image to its essential, driving to an instinctual extreme the mind's attraction to things "Stretched on the floor," or that "trail along the floor." Yet these lines also retain from the poem's conscious, ordering function the attempt at self-definition—"I should have been"—as well as the notion of dual identity, "A pair."

This five-line interlude ending on "the floors of silent seas" forms an encapsulated version of the remainder of the poem, in which the frustrated effort to establish purposive discourse leads once again to withdrawal downward and inward to a silent world of instinctual being. A return to images of distension and distracting sensuality provokes a final impulse toward violent imposition of the will—"to force the moment to its crisis"—which ends, like previous thoughts of disturbing the universe, in ruthless self-mockery. The image of decapitation parodies the theme of disconnected being and provides for at least a negative definition of the self: "I am no prophet."

By this point the tense has quietly shifted from present to past, and the speaker offers a series of prolonged interrogatives on the consequences of action not taken. While its grammatical context ("And would it have been worth it") reduces it to the contemplation of "what might have been"; the language and imagery of this passage enact with renewed intensity the recurring drama of mental conflict:

> Would it have been worth while,
> To have bitten off the matter with a smile,
> To have squeezed the universe into a ball
> To roll it towards some overwhelming question,
> To say: "I am Lazarus, come from the dead,
> Come back to tell you all, I shall tell you all."
>   (90–95)

The infinitives in this passage—*to have bitten, to have squeezed, to roll*—conform to the poem's widespread use of transitive verbs of direct action in expressing the speaker's violent impulse to combat the forces of disorder: *to murder and create, to disturb the universe, to spit out all the butt-ends, to force the moment.*

The poem's linguistic and thematic strategy consistently opposes active verbs to the passive voice which causes things to be spread out, etherized, smoothed, and stretched. It sets these infinitives against present participles, which are constantly muttering, sprawling, rubbing, scuttling, and settling. Finally, it opposes these transitive verbs to intransitive verbs which lie, linger, malinger, lean, curl, trail, wrap, slip, and sleep. A relative lack of modifiers and the absence of plural forms further distinguishes the passage cited above. By contrast the language of disordered experience, of imprecision and aimlessness, abounds in modifiers and plurals: restless nights, one-night cheap hotels, visions and revisions, the sunsets and the dooryards, and the sprinkled streets.

The structure of the imagery at this point in the poem corresponds to the thematic role played by linguistic form. To have "bitten off" the matter, in addition to its hint of blunt force, would constitute a positive reaction against endlessly idle talk; squeezing the universe into a ball would counteract the world's tendency to fall apart and to spread itself out like yellow fog; finally, the act of rolling it toward some overwhelming question at least imparts direction to the movement of the universe, even if the actual destination, like the question, remains unclear. The idea of proclaiming oneself a prophet "come back to tell you all" implies a power of linguistic discourse equal in magnitude to the physical act of squeezing the universe into a ball. Once more the idea of language joins with images of purpose, only this time in such hyperbolic fashion that the ultimate failure of discourse strikes one as inevitable: "That is not what I meant at all."

The speaker's failure to master language—"It is impossible to say just what I mean!"—leads in this case not to a statement on the inadequacy of words themselves, but rather reflects upon the speaker's own impotence. In a poem so obsessed with problems of speech and definition, to have failed with words is to have lost the war on the inarticulate: the speaker as heroic Lazarus or Prince Hamlet is suddenly reduced to the stature of an attendant lord, "Full of high sentence, but a bit obtuse." The old man with rolled-up trouser bottoms has shrunk from his former size. Paradoxically, this diminution of the outer self—the part of the mind concerned with imposing order on experience—brings about a corresponding expansion of the inner self.

In the same essay where Eliot locates the beginnings of a poem in an unknown, dark "psychic material" that is put into form by the conscious mind, he allows for a secondary resurgence of the unconscious that arises from the very process of poetic composition: "the frame, once chosen, within which the author has elected to work, may itself evoke other psychic material; and then, lines of poetry may come into being, not from the original impulse, but from a secondary stimulation of the unconscious mind."[9] The mental forces at work in Eliot's description of the poetic process serve as an analogy to the conflicts besetting the speaker in *Prufrock*. The speaker is a failed poet in terms of his inability to "murder" existing structures in order to "create" anew; he finds it impossible to say what he wants to say. In the "secondary stimulation of the unconscious mind" that occurs at this point, he partly abandons and partly resolves the struggle of form and matter; the integration of the psyche remains at best incomplete.

The image of walking upon the beach reveals a mind on the periphery of consciousness, wavering between the temptations of imagination—"I have heard the mermaids singing"—and the lingering feelings of isolation and inadequacy—"I do not think that they will sing to me." These lines recall the sense of exclusion experienced in hearing "the music from a farther room"; but the mind now is poised for flight, not confrontation. The images move outward and away—"riding seaward"—before plunging downward and inward again to the "chambers of the sea."

The final six lines of *Prufrock* create an order of the imagination that rivals the order of conscious intellect sought earlier in the poem. Whereas the speaker had earlier attempted to impose an external meaning upon the material of his psychic experience, i.e., a form not necessarily arising out of the properties of the material itself, here the form of the material takes shape as it develops from within:[10] "I have seen them riding seaward on the waves / Combing the white hair of the waves blown back / When the wind blows the water white and black." Elizabeth Drew writes that these lines provide a glimpse of "a life rhythm nor distraction. The "lingering" in the chambers of the sea[13] escapes the suggestion of malignant inertia implicit in a lingering yellow smoke or a malingering evening; on the contrary, it actually glorifies the speaker and comes close to overturning the ironic self-definition reached in an earlier context: "Am an attendant lord." The resolution of earlier tension extends even to the grammatical level, as the last few lines change a distinguishing "you and I" to an indefinite "we" and erase any thematic opposition between active and passive voice, transitive and intransitive verbs.

The absence of such tensions in the closing passage, however, signals escape as much as resolution. The problem of how one should presume, of how purpose and discourse can prevail over the aimless and inarticulate, remains unanswered after all. In his essay which sets the ordering function of poetic composition against disordered psychic material, Eliot writes: "All that matters is that in the end the voices should be heard in harmony."[14] The discords sounded early in the poem finally modulate into a third voice that ignores the score and sings in a different key. To alter the metaphor, the mind has turned back and descended the stair to its own Atlantis in a movement familiar to readers of Romantic poetry.

Northrop Frye writes of metaphorical direction in Coleridge's and Shelley's distinction between the mechanical and the organic:

> The mechanical being characteristic of ordinary experience, it is found particularly in the world "outside"; the superior or organic world is consequently "inside," and although it is still called superior or higher, the natural metaphorical direction of the inside world is downward, into the profounder depths of consciousness.[15]

In Eliot this organic world lies outward and away as well as downward and inward, thus reinforcing the motive of evasion that the poem as a whole imputes to this flight of the imagination. The sensibility informing the poem appears torn between recognizing the superiority of this inner world and relegating it to the level of nonbeing. The final line returns as from a dream to the jarring world of human voices, but it is impossible to say whether the dream issues from gates of ivory or of horn. Intellect and imagination have battled to a standoff.

where living creatures delight spontaneously in their natura
vironment, mastering it and being carried along with its
energies."[11] In these lines of the poem the relations are thos
correspondence rather than opposition or imposition: merma
waves, and wind fuse to form an organic whole. Linguistic st
ture as well as the nature of the image supports this noti
when "hair" substitutes for "foam," for example, it blurs the
tinction between mermaids and waves. A network of consonar
and assonance creates a further form of interrelation among c
ferent parts of the text and accounts largely for the lyrical qual
of these lines: *w*aves, *w*hite, *w*ind, *w*ater, *w*e; *bl*own, *b*ack, *bl*ov
*bl*ack; *sea*-girls, wr*ea*thed, *sea*weed.

Considered apart from the deflating final line, the closing pa
sage resolves in some ways the tensions informing the poem u
to this point. Earlier images of enclosure, for example, serve
only to mark off one area of aimless activity from another: "I
the room the women come and go." But here the chambers o
the sea, rather than functioning as dividing or confining struc
tures, provide an image of intimacy that avoids any tension be
tween container and contained. In the poetics of Bachelard, these
chambers share with other images of interior space the function
of providing shelter for oneiric elements of the imagination:

> *Si l'on donne à toutes ces retraites leur fonction qui fut d'abriter
> les songes, on peut dire . . . qu'il existe pour chacun de nous une
> maison onirique, une maison du souvenir-songe, perdue dans
> l'ombre d'un au-delà passé vrai. Elle est . . . la crypte de la maison
> natale.*[12]

Bachelard's theory makes it possible for us to identify this imagery with that "unknown, dark, psychic material" where Eliot
locates the poet's primary inspiration.

The sea-girls "wreathed with seaweed" in these chambers re-
mind one of "arms that are braceleted" or of women wrapped in
shawls, but the image now suggests sexual union rather than distraction. It enters into its own form of order rather than acting
as an agent of disorder to a mind seeking verbal, intellectual
meaning. In the same manner the light-brown hair and white
arms that led to digression now are reintegrated in the "white
hair" of the waves—an image representing neither stated purpose

2

The warring factions of Eliot's sensibility, brought into direct confrontation in *Prufrock*, lie scattered throughout the other poems of his first volume of verse (*Prufrock and Other Observations*, 1917). *Portrait of a Lady* (written 1910)[16] juxtaposes the formless smoke and fog of a December afternoon with the insipid preciosity of a drawing-room conversation, this time starting with Chopin instead of Michelangelo. Like his counterpart in *Prufrock*, the visitor here needs to muster all his courage just to mount the stairs. By remaining "self-possessed" he fends off the lady's overbearing attempts to arouse in him an emotional response, but his self-imposed isolation renders him essentially inarticulate: he must cry like a parrot or chatter like an ape to find expression, "not knowing what to feel or if I understand." The speaker demonstrates a latent capacity for imagination, triggered by some worn-out common song "with the smell of hyacinths across the garden"; but the ordering intellect inevitably steps in to question the validity of the experience: "Are these ideas right or wrong?" The *Preludes* (1910–12) elaborate on the theme of a disordered consciousness represented by images of fragmentation and impurity ("the burnt-out ends of smoky days"), then suddenly yield to the confessional mode. The fancies that "curl around these images" recall the smoke that curls about the house in *Prufrock*; but here the poem drives deeper into the psyche, to the unformed vision of "some infinitely gentle / Infinitely suffering thing." This octopus or angel proves too much to handle, however, and the poem returns to an easier, more cynical response: "Wipe your hand across your mouth, and laugh." The closing image of women "gathering fuel in vacant lots" provides a stunning metaphor for the *bricolage* of composition Eliot practices in these poems, a process only occasionally disturbed by the intrusion of visionary experience of the kind that ends *Prufrock*.

In the poet's attempt to establish meaning out of his chaotic world of fragmentation, distension, inarticulateness, and isolation, the kind of intellectual order that can be described in terms of architectural structure invariably proves inadequate: whispering lunar incantations "dissolve the floors of memory / And all its clear relations, / Its divisions and precisions" (*Rhapsody on a*

Windy Night). The kind of order that creates an organic fusion of its elements—"Her hair over her arms and her arms full of flowers"—continually challenges the intellect for supremacy, but remains limited in terms of its actual relevance to experience. Where a more purely Romantic poet might have elevated the material of *La Figlia che Piange* to an ideal level, Eliot treats it as a series of mere "cogitations" that "amaze." The "submarine and profound" laughter of *Mr. Apollinax* (1915) plunges us, as in *Prufrock*, into the silent waters of the psyche; but even in this poem the speaker shares something of his hosts' mistrust of Apollinax: this foetus is "irresponsible."

After *Prufrock* no single poem sets a stage large enough to accommodate the full drama of Eliot's mental action until *Gerontion* was written in 1919. Stead writes that in *Gerontion* the "gentle youthful aspirations of *Prufrock* have passed through fulfillment into some unimagined horror in which all desire that issues as action is seen as destructive."[17] One could, of course, question the characterization of the aspirations in Prufrock as "gentle"; but more important for our purposes is the fact that in terms of mental action, the speaker in *Gerontion* comes far from fulfilling the aspirations of his counterpart in *Prufrock*: he faces the same conflicts, despite his wider experience and greater suffering.

The minds informing both *Prufrock* and *Gerontion* recognize the limitations of familiar intellectual structures and seek a form of order or knowledge beyond these structures. In both poems this process reaches an impasse, causing a retreat into the limitless world of imaginative vision. The conscious search for order inevitably fails, partly because what it seeks is only a higher form of intellectual order: the mind which rolls "the universe into a ball" merely imposes an external meaning, rather than discovering an inner order of the universe. In the same way, the mind that looks for meaning to a devouring Christ-as-tiger again seeks the external imposition of order. The defining intellect remains prisoner to its own structures. Thus, in terms of the psychological conflicts reflected in their language and imagery, *Prufrock* and *Gerontion* are very nearly the same poem.

In *Gerontion*, as in *Prufrock*, the conscious desire to create order out of disorder is represented by images of purposive action opposing images of aimlessness. The dialectical struggle between these two kinds of movement finally gives over to the impulse for flight. The tension observed in *Prufrock* between dreamlike hebetude and the idea of forceful action arises in the very opening lines of *Gerontion,* where the passive "Being read to" and "waiting" contrast with the active "heaving a cutlass" and "fought." As in *Prufrock,* violence here acquires a positive value where it can be seen as destroying the forces of disorder, thus the devouring Christ-tiger and the later detonation of De Bailhache, Fresca, and Mrs. Cammel "whirled / Beyond the circuit of the shuddering Bear / In fractured atoms." A violent undercurrent in this poem threatens an already "decayed house" with demolition.

But at the beginning of the poem at least, such action exists only in the form of negative speculation. Not having fought in the warm rain is like not being Prince Hamlet in the way it provides a kind of self-definition that conforms to the poem's own expressions of aimlessness or disorder: disease, decay, random profusion, and isolation. One of the symbolist qualities of the poem lies in the interconnectedness of its images: things do not remain discrete in this network of consciousness. The goat that coughs, the woman who sneezes, and the blistered, patched, and peeled "owner" all form semantic links with words like "marsh," "flies," "Spawned," and "depraved May" in the sense that understands disease not only as decay but also as the disordered proliferation of life. The random profusion extends even to the inanimate "Rocks, moss, stone-crop, iron, merds" (where the succession of spondees creates an imitative harmony).

Eliot's symbolic use of the house in *Gerontion* conforms to his general practice of comparing architectural to mental structures. Kenner sees the house as representing not only a habitation but also the withered family stock, the European family, the Mind of Europe, the body, and finally the brain.[18] The notion of the house as the mind of the speaker partly identifies the owner of the house, "the Jew," with the speaker himself. The traditional literary role of the Jew as wanderer or "outsider" corresponds to the themes of aimlessness and isolation in *Gerontion:* the mind wanders down "cunning passages" and "contrived corridors"; its sense of isolation is conveyed in the statement, "I have no ghosts," and in the exclusion from "your closer contact" or from the obscure rituals of "the next room." In a crucial symbolic sense, then, the speaker *is* the Jew, the exile.

This interpretation tends to support Bornstein's theory of Eliot's anti-Semitism (see, for example, the "Chicago Semite Viennese" in *Burbank with a Baedeker: Bleistein with a Cigar*) as a response to "feared forces within himself."[19] In Eliot's critical writings, as well as in his verse, he systematically sought others as objects for his fears of rootlessness and exile. A letter Eliot wrote to Herbert Read (April 23, 1928) is worth quoting for the light it sheds on his sensibility:

> Some day I want to write an essay about the point of view of an American who wasn't an American, because he was born in the South and went to school in New England as a small boy with a nigger drawl, but who wasn't a southerner in the South because his people were northerners in a border state and looked down on all southerners and Virginians, and who so was never anything anywhere and who therefore felt himself to be more a Frenchman than an American and more an Englishman than a Frenchman and yet felt that the USA up to a hundred years ago was a family extension.[20]

One sees here the psychological condition treated satirically in a poem like *"Mélange adultère de tout."*

A mind prey to such uncertainty naturally looks beyond the confusion of its own world for agents of meaning and order, however dimly they may be perceived. But in *Gerontion*, as in *Prufrock*, the failure of language frustrates the search for meaning. Signs, either verbal or prophetic, are taken for mere wonders. The true miracle of Christ's coming as the *Verbum infans*, which causes Bishop Lancelot Andrewes to marvel at the divine paradox of "the Word an Infant . . . The Word, and not able to speak a word,"[21] is distorted by the poem and converted to a statement of the inarticulate and isolated nature of verbal expression: "The word within a word, unable to speak a word."

This theme of aborted discourse carries through the mysterious "whispers" of secret ritual to the figure of History, which "issues, deceives with whispering ambitions" (here the sibilants actually imitate the whispering). Subversion of discourse corresponds to aimless movement: the walking all night in the next room ("In the room the women come and go"), the senseless caressing, bowing and shifting, the vacant shuttles weaving the wind. The poem extends this disorder to existing forms of knowledge, and treats the subject of History simultaneously in spatial, sexual, and intellectual terms. The labyrinthine nature of History's passages and corridors recalls the streets of *Prufrock*, complete with their "insidious intent," and provides an architectural setting for the "wilderness of mirrors" that appears later.

The characterization of History as a female figure ingeniously compares the desire for meaning to sexual desire, and in a manner more complex than *Prufrock* relates the problems of knowledge to sexual disorder. A semantic chain of sexual connotation connects "cunning" passages (with its latent pun) to supple confusions, craving, passion, propagation, unnatural vices, and the act of fathering. The sexual theme is tied syntactically to a discussion of thought, attention, memory, and belief, thereby equating the failure of sexual intercourse with that of intellectual discourse. History "Gives too late / What's not believed in, or is still believed, / In memory only, reconsidered passion." One loses passion in memory just as one loses terror in inquisition: the knowledge imposes a pattern, and falsifies. The mind's impotence lies in its failure to successfully know, to define.

Paradoxically the entire process of comparing intellectual to sexual disorder is motivated by the repeated imperative "Think now," "Think," "Think at last," as if the power to transcend the limitations of knowledge lay in the intellectual act itself. The imperative mood reflects the conscious resolution of a mind that "has not made this show purposelessly" and is determined to "meet you upon this honestly." It has deliberately avoided stirring up the forces of madness, which in a poem like *Rhapsody on a Windy Night* produce a woman whose eye "Twists like a crooked pin."

The concern here for problems of thought, action, and discourse conforms to linguistic structures that generally distinguish the poem's central passages. Beginning with the question "After such knowledge, what forgiveness?" the poem shifts from thirty lines of direct declaratives to a long series of interrogatives, imperatives, and subjunctives. In terms of mental action, the syntactical shift reflects a movement from weary resignation to volition and "inquisition," as the mind struggles in vain against its own tendency to submit to the "windy spaces." The intensity of the struggle revives the verbs of violent action—"forced," "shaken," "springs," "devours"—which served the poem's opening only for the purpose of ironic contrast: "Nor . . . heaving a cutlass / Bitten by flies, fought." The assertion of the intellectual faculty sacrifices the concrete imagery of the opening passages— the rocks and merds, the "one hand on the door"—to the language of abstraction: of knowledge, forgiveness, vanities, confusions. The opening passages exhibit a rich texture of assonance and consonance, as well as a controlled rhythm of stresses and caesurae that creates at least an "auditory illusion" of coherence:[22]

Sneézes at évening, / póking the peévish / gútter

But where the poem starts asking questions and trying to "think," the rhythm sprawls and the texture deteriorates into frenetic repetition: "gives, gives . . . giving . . . Gives too late . . . Gives too soon"; "Think at last," "Think at last"; "terror, terror"; "I have lost . . . I have lost. . . ."

The linguistic form of these central passages reflects the frustration of mind in which statements of purpose disintegrate rapidly into the imagery of loss and isolation: "I that was near your heart was removed therefrom." The idea of isolation extends to the separation of the senses from the brain, thus ultimately reducing mental action to the random profusion of empty gestures—"multiply variety"—severed from actual consequence. This separation constitutes one more step in the gradual withdrawal of the self from the field of meaningful action, in proportion as the mind encounters successive failures in its attempts to create order.

After its beginning concern for the larger questions of history, ambition, virtue, and heroism, *Gerontion* retreats to a problem more limited in scope: that of contact with a single human being. The withdrawal inward, like a series of doors closing one after the other, continues to the point where the mind no longer connects to its own "sight, smell, hearing, taste, and touch." The radically diminished nature of the self leads in Prufrockian fashion to an ironic contrast between the "thousand small deliberations" of the mind and the cosmic dimensions of time and the universe. As if reaching a breaking point, the frustrations inherent in such an evaluation of the self finally yield, as in *Prufrock*, to escape into images of flight ("Gull against the wind"), purity ("White feathers in the snow"), and the plunge downward and inward ("the Gulf claims").

The lyrical energy released in these lines about the gull and the sea removes them from the earlier dialectical struggle between chaos and order. The intellect momentarily steps aside for an Icarian flight of the imagination that echoes not only Yeats's seaborne bird "balanced on the air,"[23] but also Mallarmé's sea birds *"ivres d'être parmi l'écume inconnue et les cieux"* in *Brise marine*. The "windy straits" recall the "passages" of history and the "windy knob" earlier in the poem, but here the images are transformed into a vision of beauty recaptured from inquisition. The freedom of "running" on the Horn contrasts with earlier uses of the present participle: passively "waiting" for rain, violently "heaving" a cutlass, aimlessly "bowing" and "caressing." The doubly pure white-on-white of feathers in the snow removes us from the impure world of "depraved" May and "adulterated" passion.

The final passage also effects an escape from earlier syntactical structures in the poem, dispensing with the distinction between subject and predicate in order to present the image in its immediacy. This technique combines with a fluid rhythmical structure, unlike the stressed cadences of the poem's opening or the protracted measures of the middle section, to give the passage what Eliot called (in the case of Poe and Mallarmé)[24] an "incantatory" quality. The primary rhythmical device here of the trochaic foot followed by an anapest (as in "chambers of the sea") produces the "running" sound of "running on the Horn," "Gull against the wind," "feathers in the snow," "driven by the Trades." Sheer rhythmical momentum carries this device into the poem's closing utterance—"Tenants of the house, / Thoughts of a dry brain in a dry season"—which undercuts the vision, seeking to deny its validity. Either fearing the freedom of the imagination or wearying of the energy it requires, the poem returns us to the confines of the house, to a world in which the struggle for order takes place entirely within the context of a defining intellect. The attempt to treat the imaginative vision as only one more form of disorder does not wholly succeed, given the internal order of the vision itself as well as its independent origin within the mind of the speaker. Once more the poet battles to a draw with his octopus or angel.

This interpretation departs from traditional readings of the poem in making qualitative distinctions between the speaker's desperate search for rational coherence and his sudden abandonment of this search in a moment of nonrational inspiration. Grover Smith takes the poem entirely at face value when he writes, "In *Gerontion* . . . an old man's lost power to love and his lost hope of spiritual rebirth create a symbol of sterility and paralysis."[25] The statement is plausible as far as it goes, but it reflects an approach to the poem that overlooks the underlying movements against sterility and paralysis as well as the tensions between different kinds of mental action. Smith later adds: "The cold snows of Belle Isle and Cape Horn . . . are in their turn a symbol of the cold death of the spirit; the white feathers of the courageous sea bird an ironic symbol of cowardice and loss."[26] Here he agrees too readily with the arid logic of the poem's final line and ignores the way in which the lyrical passage attests to the survival of imaginative power even in a mind that mistrusts it.

Like *Prufrock* then, *Gerontion* gives voice to a poetic sensibility torn in its loyalties between meaning and vision, between the poet's task of bringing order to life and his privilege of soaring or plunging beyond its limits. Each of these poems portrays the drama of a mind struggling violently with the elements of a world that invariably frustrates the attempt to act purposefully or to elicit response from another being. In such a world the aimless quality of movement and the inarticulate nature of expression are tied inextricably to images of fragmentation, randomness, isolation, and distension.

Finding itself a prisoner of its own labyrinthine structures, the mind strives to overcome this condition in forms of mental action that serve only to strengthen the prison walls—like the man trapped in quicksand, whose efforts to free himself only mire him more deeply. Thus the intellect, recognizing the aimless nature of "decisions and revisions which a minute will reverse," can only contemplate imposing its own kind of order on a larger scale, in the form of omniscient prophecy or devouring epiphany. *Geron-*

tion treats this notion portentously, whereas *Prufrock* considers it ironically; but in each case the result is the same: external sources fail to bring the desired sense of meaning.

The failure of meaning leads the speaker to question his own identity, to the point where the principle of individuation—the sense of *I* versus *other*—is suspended completely in a moment of vision. The sudden unveiling of an ecstatic world of flight, purity, and correspondence offers refuge from the war with disorder; but the ultimate return to self-consciousness repudiates the dynamic order of the visionary world. Each poem returns in circular fashion to its own beginning, and leaves us, as before, "waiting for rain."

NOTES

1. T. S. Eliot, *The Three Voices of Poetry* (Cambridge: National Book League, 1955), p. 21.

2. Robert Langbaum, *The Poetry of Experience: The Dramatic Monologue in Modern Literary Tradition* (London: Chatto & Windus, 1957), p. 104.

3. Elisabeth Schneider, *T. S. Eliot: The Pattern in the Carpet* (Berkeley: University of California Press, 1975), p. 26.

4. Hugh Kenner, *The Invisible Poet: T. S. Eliot* (New York: Obolensky, 1959), p. 125.

5. Bornstein, *Transformations of Romanticism*, p. 131.

6. T. S. Eliot, *Collected Poems 1909– 1962* (New York: Harcourt, Brace & World, 1970), hereafter abbreviated as *CP* and cited in the text.

7. The identity of this "you" has puzzled a number of commentators, e.g., George Williamson, *A Reader's Guide to T. S. Eliot*, 2d ed. (New York: Farrar, Straus & Giroux, 1966), p. 59.

8. Kenner, *The Invisible Poet*, p. 36.

9. Eliot, *Three Voices of Poetry*, p. 21.

10. Samuel Taylor Coleridge, "Mechanic and Organic Form," in *Shakespearean Criticism*: "The form is mechanic when on any given material we impress a pre-determined form, not necessarily arising out of the properties of the material, as when to a mass of wet clay we give whatever shape we wish it to retain when hardened. The organic form, on the other hand, is innate; it shapes as it develops itself from within, and the fullness of its development is one and the same with the perfection of its outward form." Quoted in David Perkins, ed., *English Romantic Writers* (New York: Harcourt, Brace & World, 1967), p. 500.

11. Elizabeth Drew, *T. S. Eliot: The Design of His Poetry* (New York: Charles Scribner's Sons, 1949), p. 35.

12. Gaston Bachelard, *La Poétique de l'espace* (Paris: Presses universitaires de France, 1957), p. 33.

13. Compare Nerval's "J'ai rêvé dans la grotte où nage la sirène," in *El Desdichado*, a poem that offers several thematic and structural parallels to Eliot's work.

14. Eliot, *Three Voices of Poetry*, p. 23.

15. Northrop Frye, ed., *Romanticism Reconsidered* (New York: Columbia University Press, 1963), p. 8.

16. Dates of composition are provided in B. C. Southam, *A Guide to the Selected Poems of T. S. Eliot* (New York: Harcourt, Brace & World, 1969).

17. Stead, *The New Poetic*, p. 157.

18. Kenner, *The Invisible Poet*, p. 125.

19. Bornstein, *Transformations of Romanticism*, p. 149.

20. Quoted in Stephen Spender, *T. S. Eliot* (New York: Penguin, 1975), p. 16.

21. Quoted by Eliot in *Selected Essays*, p. 307.

22. Cf. Kenner, *The Invisible Poet*, p. 125.

23. W. B. Yeats, *Collected Poems* (New York: Macmillan, 1974), p. 181. Cited in Bornstein, *Transformations of Romanticism*, p. 137.

24. T. S. Eliot, "Note sur Mallarmé et Poe," *Nouvelle revue française* 14 (1926).

25. Grover Smith, *T. S. Eliot's Poetry and Plays* (Chicago: University of Chicago Press, 1974), p. 57.

26. Ibid., p. 65.

CHAPTER TWO

The Inner Xanadu of The Waste Land

IN THE PERIOD of poetic development that culminates in the publication of *The Waste Land* (1922), T. S. Eliot strengthens the formal limitations on his verse as if searching for ways to contain an increasingly unruly imagination. The purely imagistic free verse of the *Preludes* (published 1917) and the casual prose-poem form of *Hysteria* (also 1917) no longer seem possible for the author of *Ara Vos Prec* (1920). The new poems of this volume either maintain the dramatic form with growing danger to the coherence of the personae (*Gerontion, Dans le restaurant*) or combine ironic tone with turgid vocabulary in the highly stylized quatrain form: "Polyphiloprogenitive / The sapient sutlers of the Lord" (*CP*, p. 47). In *The Waste Land* Eliot's persona and poetic form, as if cracking under the strain of some inner turbulence, literally break apart into a variety of voices and meters in a process accompanied by the actual fragmentation of language.

The general proliferation of Eliot's personae creates a poem that seems to take off in several directions at once; one can nonetheless identify two main currents in the poem that correspond to a basic division in the poet's consciousness. One aspect of Eliot's consciousness embraces a modern version of the medieval process of *askesis* or the Negative Way; having abandoned earlier · attempts to conquer experience by means of sheer intellectual force, it pursues a disordered world toward a state of final disintegration where symbols of external authority offer the only form of meaning. The other main current gets in the way of this process by exploring the poet's visionary Xanadu—an inner world of purity and fusion with nature. Critics have traditionally failed to

recognize this or any analogous conflict in the poem because of
their overreliance on sources like the Grail legend and Elizabethan drama as guides to reading *The Waste Land*. In their eager-
ness to establish narrative coherence on one level, they overlook
opposing movements at other levels of the poem.

My own approach to *The Waste Land* departs from this tradition in three important ways: First, it treats the poem as a
stage for the interaction of differing levels of consciousness rather
than defining the poem in terms of a coherent "statement" or a
conscious "point of view" on experience.[1] Second, it groups elements of the text according to their common structural qualities
rather than according to their place in a supposed narrative sequence. Finally, it sees the poem's ending as a climactic shatter-
ing of consciousness into psychic and linguistic incoherence
rather than as a partial realization of experiential unity.

A better definition of the opposing movements in the poem
may come from the way Eliot as a critic handles them in the
works of other authors. In Dostoyevsky he finds the willful pursuit of disorder toward a state where salvation can only be offered
by a force from without:

> Dostoyevsky's point of departure is always a human brain in a
> human environment, and the "aura" is simply the continuation
> of the quotidian experience of the brain into seldom explored ex-
> tremities of torture. Because most people are too unconscious of
> their own suffering to suffer much, this continuation appears fan-
> tastic. But Dostoyevsky begins with the real world, as Beyle does;
> he only pursues reality further in a different direction.[2]

This passage describes the way in which Eliot's own poem takes
the fragile rituals of daily reality—speech, time, seasonal change,
copulation—and subjects them to a disintegration that verges on
madness: "I can connect / Nothing with nothing."

This function of the poem coexists with another, somewhat
incompatible, artistic concern that Eliot describes in a discussion
of Coleridge's *Kubla Khan*: "The imagery of that fragment, certainly, whatever its origins in Coleridge's readings, sank to the
depths of Coleridge's feeling, was saturated, transformed there—
'those are pearls that were his eyes'—and brought up into day-
light again."[3] Eliot characteristically locates the origins of inspira-

tion downward and inward in what Northrop Frye calls, in the
case of the Romantic poets, the "mind's internal heaven."[4]
Where the early poems offered us only fleeting glimpses of this
inner world, *The Waste Land* opens windows on it through the
language and imagery of purity and organic unity. This is the
world of the hyacinth garden, of the children *"chantant dans la
coupole,"* of "Inexplicable splendour of Ionian white and gold,"
of "aethereal rumours." In their efforts to derive a narrative sequence or a coherent statement of belief from the poem, critics
have generally incorporated such passages into the poem's general ethos of disillusionment and decay. By doing so, however,
they overlook the ways in which this inner world, by remaining
intact, actually frustrates the appeal to external authority for deliverance from the chaos of the waste land.

The presiding consciousness of *The Waste Land* finds itself in
a situation analogous to that of the divided speaker in Yeats's "A
Dialogue of Self and Soul" (published 1933), where a judgmental
Soul demands, but cannot compel, renunciation and purgatorial
ascent from a Self obsessed with the earthly joys of imagination.
Eliot himself thought little of what he called Yeats's "sojourn in
the world of imagination." He wrote, in a review of *The Wild
Swans at Coole* (1919): "[Yeats] is worn out not with dreams,
but with the vain effort to master them and submit them to his
own creative energy. He has not subdued them nor built a new
world from them; he has merely followed them like will-o'-the-
wisps away from the world he knew."[5] This tells us less about
Yeats than about Eliot, whose own work reflects a crucial ambivalence toward the world of imagination. On one hand, Eliot's
poems convey what he calls in Stendhal and Flaubert a "discon-
tent with the inevitable inadequacy of actual living to the passionate capacity"[6] of imagination; on the other hand, they reveal
an unwilling attraction to the order of imagination as a superior
form of being: "By this, and this only, we have existed." Eliot's
own difficulty in subduing his vision ultimately leads him to the
ascetic form of Christianity for which *The Waste Land* clears the
way.

The following discussion of *The Waste Land* takes two parts:
part 1 examines a series of specific passages scattered throughout
the poem and joins them through the notion of convergence or

"constellation" of images[7]—images which hold semantic or spatial elements in common. In this way images of purity (childhood, whiteness, gold, the garden) combine with images of elevation and descent to define a visionary inner world into which the poet soars or plunges in escaping the waste land's surface chaos. This section also demonstrates the ambiguity of these passages in relation to their immediate context in the poem. Part 2 leaves this inner world of imagination, and interprets Eliot's images of destruction and fragmentation in terms of an ultimate "search for authenticity" which has analogues both in medieval Christian mysticism and in the existential philosophy of Eliot's contemporaries. The latent conflict between these two main currents culminates in the Upanishadic section of "What the Thunder Said," where allusions to the speaker's inner vision frustrate his response to moral imperatives delivered from above.

1

In the actual text of *The Waste Land* the material of the poet's organic inner world enjoys a thematic and formal autonomy that in some ways resists assimilation to its surrounding context. The poem opens with seven lines of figurative language that compare nature to mental process—"memory and desire," "forgetful snow"—while establishing a series of semantically opposed terms: *cruel* v. *April, lilacs* v. *dead land, memory* v. *desire, winter* v. *warm, life* v. *dried tubers*. The sudden shift to a series of longer, more fluid lines with medial caesurae signals a corresponding thematic shift that removes us from the dialectical oppositions of the opening passage:

> Summer surprised us, coming over the Starnbergersee
> With a shower of rain; we stopped in the colonnade,
> And went on in sunlight, into the Hofgarten,
> And drank coffee, and talked for an hour.
> Bin gar keine Russin, stamm' aus Litauen, echt deutsch.
> And when we were children, staying at the arch-duke's,
> My cousin's, he took me out on a sled,
> And I was frightened. He said, Marie,
> Marie, hold on tight. And down we went.
>
> (8–15)

The simple and direct language here contrasts with the epideictic style of the opening. Its casual intimacy conveys a sense of well-being not unlike that of the fishmen in part 3 lounging at noon, while the imagery of enclosure, childhood innocence, and flight (or freedom of movement in general) ties this passage to the larger theme of imaginative order that develops throughout the poem.

D. E. S. Maxwell misses the point of this scene when he tells us that Marie "is separated not only from the life of a nation, but also from that other natural unit, the family, for her memories involve neither father nor mother, only a holiday at a cousin's."[8] This rationalizes the lines rather than acknowledges what for most readers would be an intuitive understanding of them. Like many critics, Maxwell overlooks the lyrical undercurrents of such passages in an effort to reconcile them with more obvious movements in the poem.

One could say that the Maxwell reading is justified by the sudden movement of the poem from innocence to weary banality, from the particular to the general: "In the mountains, there you feel free. / I read, much of the night, and go south in the winter." But these lines act more as a response to the lyrical scene than as a component of it. Like Gerontion's evaluation of his ecstatic vision as "Thoughts of a dry brain in a dry season," they seek to discredit the privileged moment without actually violating its essential integrity.

A dozen lines later the poem announces another sudden illumination of the imagination's inner world as the foreboding language of the prophet gives way to the young sailor's song that opens *Tristan und Isolde:*

> *Frisch weht der Wind*
> *Der Heimat zu*
> *Mein Irisch Kind*
> *Wo weilest du?*
> 'You gave me hyacinths first a year ago;
> 'They called me the hyacinth girl.'
> —Yet when we came back, late, from the hyacinth garden,
> Your arms full, and your hair wet, I could not
> Speak, and my eyes failed, I was neither
> Living nor dead, and I knew nothing,

Looking into the heart of light, the silence.
Oed' und leer das Meer.

(31–42)

The rhythmical shift provided by the sailor's song announces a revival of the thematic concerns of the Marie scene. Both passages move us from an expanse of water into a garden, where the speaker shares some intimate experience with a female figure, involving use of the first person pronoun: "we stopped. . . . we came back. . . ." The *Irisch Kind* and the hyacinth girl evoke the innocence of "when we were children." The sexual overtones of Marie's sleigh ride come to fruition in the image of "Your arms full, and your hair wet," recalling *La Figlia che Piange* with "Her hair over her arms and her arms full of flowers." The speaker's ambivalence toward this vision of fulfillment and purity arises out of his futile effort to define it in terms of speech, sight, and knowledge: "I could not / Speak, and my eyes failed, I was neither / Living nor dead, and I knew nothing." The line-break before *Speak* imitates formally the theme of the inarticulate. More important, the concern with discursive forms of defining the experience detrays a desire for intellectual order that opposes the essentially intuitive quality of the vision.

This conflict between a naming, defining mind and an imagination that follows its own rules of order makes the scene in the hyacinth garden a metaphor for the basic problem of the artist. It is probably Eliot's obsession with this problem in his own work that leads to his critical misjudgment of Yeats in 1919, in whom "nothing remains of the sweet world of imagination. Mr. Yeats has made the tragic mistake of thinking that to contemplate it was sufficient. Had he been a great poet he would have made it his own, by forcing it into the fetters of speech."[9] That final metaphor goes a long way toward revealing Eliot's fundamental attitude toward the imagination and its relation to language: the imagination is essential to great poetry, but the poem must keep it contained and subdued, like a wild bird in a cage.

In "The Burial of the Dead" the speaker's own failure to master his imagination leads to despair as he shifts from "looking into" the heart of light to looking out onto a desolate and empty sea. The in-out movement parallels the metaphorical direction of

"coming back" from the hyacinth garden; the desire for knowledge expels the mind from its inner Eden. *Oed' und leer das
Meer*: just as in Wagner's opera this song awakens Tristan only
to hasten his death, so also in Eliot's poem it brings us back to the
circular death-in-life of Madame Sosostris's world and "crowds of
people, walking round in a ring."

Madame Sosostris's monologue is interrupted at one point by
a parenthetical exclamation that does not quite conform to the
context of sententious divination: "(Those are pearls that were
his eyes. Look!)." Once again the look is directed, if only for a
moment, downward and inward to the world of the drowned
sailor. The original drafts to the poem show that Ezra Pound
wanted the line left out.[10] By keeping the line, however, Eliot
preserved a reference to the "rich and strange" undersea world
explored as a source of vitality in poems like *Prufrock* and *Mr.
Apollinax*, and occasionally used in Eliot's prose as a metaphor
for the "depths" of a poet's feeling.[11] The presence of this "submarine and profound" realm in Eliot's poetic universe places him
squarely in the Romantic tradition of Atlantis, which Frye describes as "the sunken island kingdom which we can rediscover by
draining the 'Sea of Time and Space' off the top of our mind."[12]
Thus *Prometheus Unbound* celebrates, in terms later to emerge
in Eliot's imagery, the reappearance of Atlantis upon Prometheus's liberation:

> Behold the Nereids under the green sea,
> Their wavering limbs borne on the wind-like stream,
> Their white arms lifted o'er their streaming hair
> With garlands pied and starry sea-flower crowns,
> Hastening to grace their mighty sister's joy.
>
> (3. 2. 44–48)

Eliot's subaqueous realm is identical with his hyacinth garden:
both serve as metaphors for "our first world" of undissociated
sensibility and organic unity, a world that Eliot, unlike Shelley,
cannot reconcile with his awareness of an essentially disordered
reality.

The exclamatory interjection in the speech of Madame Sosostris resurfaces in "A Game of Chess," where a frantic dialogue

renews the poem's general concern with the problem of speech—
"Why do you never speak. Speak"—and knowledge:

> 'Do
> 'You know nothing? Do you see nothing? Do you remember
> 'Nothing?'
>   I remember
> Those are pearls that were his eyes.

(121–25)

The original drafts to this passage make explicit the identity in
the speaker's mind of the undersea world and the garden: "I remember / The hyacinth garden. Those are pearls that were his
eyes, yes!" (Pound notes, "Penelope / J.J.," in ironic reference to
Molly Bloom's affirmative soliloquy in the Penelope scene of
Ulysses).[13] In either version the speaker does not really answer his
anguished interrogator; his response is a private statement, an escape from the futility of discourse. Taken in a literal sense, the
next question, "Are you alive, or not?" may be answered by the
testimony from the hyacinth garden, "I was neither / Living nor
dead"; for the contemplation of the submerged world constitutes
a removal from the cyclical processes of life and death that characterize the surface reality of the waste land.

The "Death by Water" section further explores this notion
of the symbolic inward plunge as signifying withdrawal from
the "mere complexities" of life and death, time and space. The
drowned sailor, though "a fortnight dead," yet journeys back
toward his origins as he moves from age through youth:

> Phlebas the Phoenecian, a fortnight dead,
> Forgot the cry of gulls, and the deep sea swell
> And the profit and loss.
>   A current under sea
> Picked his bones in whispers. As he rose and fell
> He passed the stages of his age and youth
> Entering the whirlpool.

(312–18)

George Williamson, obeying the injunction to "Consider Phlebas, who was once handsome and tall as you," understands this
section primarily as a moral lesson: " 'Death by Water' brings
the Phoenecian sailor and the ultimate consequence of the lust

theme, of the fire. Now the protagonist's anticipated fate has been executed."[14] But this overlooks the tranquility of Phlebas's state, the way this passage removes us momentarily from the disorder of the waste land. Cleanth Brooks has pointed to the difference between this passage and the description of death in part 3, "bones cast in a little low dry garret / Rattled by the rat's foot only, year to year."[15] The tone of the Phlebas passage comes much closer to that of Ariel's song, "Of his bones are coral made." It is almost as if the poet, failing to heed the admonition to "Fear death by water," were instead attracted to the richness and strangeness of the notion.

One gathers some idea of the symbolic significance of the undersea theme from Eliot's use of it in other places. In *Dans le restaurant* (published 1918), a French version of "Death by Water" follows an episode that prefigures the imagery of the hyacinth garden scene:

> 'Les saules trempés, et des bourgeons sur les ronces—
> C'est là, dans une averse, qu'on s'abrite.
> J'avais sept ans, elle était plus petite.
> Elle etait toute mouillée, je lui ai donné des
>   primevères.'[16]
>   (8–11)

Sixteen lines later a current undersea carries the drowned Phoenecian far away:

> Un courant de sous-mer l'emporta tres loin,
> Le repassant aux étapes de sa vie antérieure.
>   (28–29)

The last three words allude to Baudelaire's *La Vie antérieure*,[17] in which the French poet evokes a primordial former life of *"voluptés calmes,"* where he enters into union with the elements of nature. In passages from the original drafts to *The Waste Land* this reunion involves, as in Ariel's song, a merging with the elements of the deep:

> Those are pearls that were his eyes. See!
> And the crab shelters in his stomach, the eel grows big
> And the torn algae drift above him, purple, red,
> And the sea colander.
> Still and quiet brother are you still and quiet.[18]

Apart from the way they shed light on the more obscure regions
of Eliot's sensibility, such extratextual sources simply expand
upon elements already implicit in the Phlebas scene as we know
it. These elements connect the passage semantically to themes of
depth, stillness, and original unity, which throughout the poem
point us toward the imagination's inner world.

It seems a paradox of the Romantic imagination that this inner
world of harmony and purity is so often characterized in terms of
elevation and flight; the imagination takes us upward and outward as well as downward and inward. But the two movements
do not really oppose each other in the thematic context of *The
Waste Land*. Metaphorically speaking, if the hyacinth garden
lies in the mind's internal heaven as well as in its internal Atlantis—for the Romantic there is no difference—then it matters
not whether one arrives there through ascension or descent. To
the observer who sees the heavens reflected in a dark pool, the
plunge and the ascent are one. This simply extends the familiar
notion that the Romantic poet sees Nature as a mirror reflecting
his own soul. Coleridge says in the Notebooks: "In looking at
objects of Nature, I seem rather to be seeking, as it were *asking
for*, a symbolical language for something within me that already
and forever exists, than observing anything new."[19] Unlike in
Dante, where elevation or ascent acquires an allegorical value
opposed to that of depth or descent, the two directions are reconciled in the Romantic mind. *Kubla Khan* moves through "caverns measureless to man" into a "deep romantic chasm" and finally to a sunny "dome in air." Baudelaire in *La Chevelure*
plunges into the *"noir océan"* of his lover's hair, finding there
"l'azur du ciel immense et rond."

Considered in this light, Eliot's "octopus or angel with which
the poet struggles"[20] stands for a single source of inspiration,
angel and octopus being only the light and dark sides of the
same interior moon. The angelic image of Gerontion's "Gull
against the wind" performs the same function as Prufrock's tentacular undersea world in providing an objective correlative for
the life of the imagination. Similarly, *The Waste Land* defines
its own privileged "moments of being"[21] in terms of elevation
and music as well as depth and silence. Either way offers escape
from what the poem presents as the sordid reality subject to time.

The first two verse-paragraphs of "The Fire Sermon," for example, project what William F. Lynch describes as a "flattening out of the orders of human sensibility,"[22] an attitude that reduces all forms of human experience to the lowest common denominator of ontological value. Lynch's metaphor is well-chosen, for apart from the familiar images of fragmentation and random profusion ("empty bottles, sandwich papers / Silk handkerchiefs, cardboard boxes") this passage focuses on things close to the ground, on a world of lowness (as distinguished from depth): the low damp ground, a low dry garret, the rat's foot, "They wash their feet."

Against this background the line from Verlaine bursts forth like a sudden illumination, an image recalled from another world: *"Et O ces voix d'enfants, chantant dans la coupole!"* Critics who interpret this line as merely another reference to the Grail legend overlook the way it differs qualitatively from the surrounding context. The vertical movement to the voices singing in the cupola lifts us out of the images of lowness, while it refers us, in terms of spatial orientation, to the sailor in *Tristan,* whose song (*Frisch weht der Wind*) is heard "on high, as if from the mast."[23] The shift into the French of Verlaine removes us from the language of a passage nearly devoid of latinate forms and dominated by such solid Anglo-Saxon words as *belly, wreck,* and *death.* The reference to children connects the line thematically to the hyacinth garden and the Marie scene, while the singing carries forward to another scene of music, elevation, and purity:

> 'This music crept by me upon the waters'
> And along the Strand, up Queen Victoria Street.
> O City city, I can sometimes hear
> Beside a public bar in Lower Thames Street,
> The pleasant whining of a mandoline
> And a clatter and a chatter from within
> Where fishmen lounge at noon: where the walls
> Of Magnus Martyr hold
> Inexplicable splendour of Ionian white and gold.
>
> (257–65)

In *Portrait of a Lady* the overly correct young man who is the poem's speaker keeps his countenance and remains "self-possessed,"

> Except when a street-piano, mechanical and tired
> Reiterates some worn-out common song
> With the smell of hyacinths across the garden
> Recalling things that other people have desired.
>
> (79–82)

The passage describes an involuntary attraction to a state of sympathy with one's surroundings that prefigures the way "The Fire Sermon" shifts from the typist's seduction scene into the lyrical passage introduced by the reference to Ariel's music. Although the speaker has "foresuffered all / Enacted on this same divan or bed," his vocabulary denotes a detachment from the scene of sexual disorder: "Endeavours to engage her," "encounter no defence." Like the legendary Tiresias, he stands outside the dramatic action; his role is to perceive and to foretell.

The lyrical passage, on the other hand, dissolves the barrier between subject and object in the implied harmony of speaker, music, public bar, and the walls of Magnus Martyr. To the extent that the passage fuses these various elements, the city invoked here represents a different order of consciousness from that of the "Unreal city" addressed fifty lines earlier. The speaker enters momentarily a realm of purity removed from the imperfections of a debased human world. The lounging fishmen thus resemble the sailor in an early version of "Death by Water" who "retains, even ashore, in public bars or streets / Something inhuman, clean and dignified."[24] "This music," taken in its original Shakespearean context, connects with other passages in Eliot's poem that remove us from the surface disorder of the waste land by ascending into air or plunging under water:

> The ditty does remember my drowned father.
> This is no mortal business, nor no sound
> That the earth owes. I hear it now above me.
>
> (*The Tempest*, 1. 2. 406–8)

More immediately, the elevation of the walls of Magnus Martyr raises us out of the lowly world of "One of the low," where the speaker has sat "below the wall / And walked among the lowest of the dead." The "Ionian white and gold" (with its intricate pattern of repeated vowels) provides a final chromatic contrast to "brown fog" and the "violet hour."

The poem's movement from Magnus Martyr to "The river sweats / Oil and tar" would return us to the familiar ethos of pollution and decay, but the speaker seems reluctant to relinquish his vision of purity:

> Elizabeth and Leicester
> Beating oars
> The stern was formed
> A gilded shell
> Red and gold
> The brisk swell
> Rippled both shores
> Southwest wind
> Carried down stream
> The peal of bells
> White towers
>> Weialala leia
>> Wallala leialala
>
> (279–91)

Cleanth Brooks writes that this passage "reinforces the general contrast between Elizabethan magnificence and modern sordidness." He then qualifies this by saying that "the same sterile love, emptiness of love," existed in Elizabeth's period as well.[25]

But to interpret the poem simply as a moral statement comparing past and present does injustice to the complexity of Eliot's method. In this case it overlooks the way the Elizabeth-and-Leicester passage connects symbolically to a pattern of heightened imagination throughout the poem. The "gilded shell / Red and gold" and the "White towers" match the splendour of Magnus Martyr (originally "Michael Paternoster Royal, red and white")[26] in both color and elevation. The "peal of bells" and the song of the Thames-daughters echo the music of Ariel, the mandoline, the singing in the cupola, and Wagner's sailor. The fresh wind of the sailor's song blows southwesterly here into a "brisk swell," while the exhilaration of being "Carried down stream" matches that of Marie's sleigh ride. For a poem concerned on one level with the theme of purgation, *The Waste Land* shows a remarkable appreciation for the joys of the sensual imagination.

2

In one of the more important essays on Eliot's work to appear
in recent years, William V. Spanos interprets *Sweeney Agonistes*
(1932) in terms of modern man's "search for authenticity" as it
is described by philosophers such as Kierkegaard, Karl Jaspers,
and Heidegger, whose *Sein und Zeit* appeared four years after
The Waste Land.[27] In one version of this theory, the inauthentic
life consists of a continual round of distractions from the recognition of one's own imminent death, a constant "fleeing in the
face of death." The individual becomes authentic only when
driven to a "boundary situation" (*Grenzsituation*) where he encounters death face-to-face and accepts it as "my own." According to Jaspers we react to such situations "either by obfuscations
or, if we really apprehend them, by despair and rebirth: we become ourselves by a change in our consciousness of being."[28]

From this new perspective, in which the self perceives the "unreal" nature of modern life's distractions, death comes to assume
a benign character in spite of its horror. Spanos writes, "Eliot . . .
responded to the disintegration of meaning in the modern world
by acknowledging . . . the boundary-situation as the terrain of his
poetic exploration."[29] One recognizes this theory as a modern version of the medieval concept of *askesis*, the conscious emptying
out from the soul of both discursive thought and images of sense
in purgatorial preparation for the marriage with God. Indeed, the
second epigraph to *Sweeney Agonistes* cites St. John of the Cross:
"Hence the soul cannot be possessed of the divine union, until it
has divested itself of the love of created beings." Both the medieval mystics and the modern existentialists see the confrontation of nothingness as crucial in the search for meaning in life.
Thus St. John of the Cross says in a passage that Eliot adopts in
the *Four Quartets*: "If you want to possess everything / You
must desire to possess nothing."[30]

The poet of *The Waste Land* has not yet embraced Christianity and does not necessarily have a philosophical doctrine to
expound. Nonetheless Spanos's analysis of the dramatic fragment
written ten years later allows us to see the themes of destruction
and emptiness in *The Waste Land*, as well as the appeals to a

higher authority, as necessary preludes to the poet's later spiritual development. Eliot's problem of reconciling this development to his obsession with the life of the imagination ultimately will draw him to the principle of *askesis* rather than to some other Christian discipline. From the perspective of his later work, one can see the roots of this problem in the poem of 1922.

Poems such as *Prufrock* and *Gerontion* dramatized the frustrations of the intellect in its efforts to establish meaning out of a disordered universe, but by the time of *The Waste Land* the intellect has practically given up the struggle: knowledge amounts to nothing more than "a heap of broken images," while discourse is reduced to fragmented utterance:

> Twit twit twit
> Jug jug jug jug jug jug
> So rudely forc'd.
> Tereu

In the poem's technique of extending "the quotidian experience of the brain into seldom explored extremities of torture,"[31] it repeatedly approaches a boundary situation where the face of nothingness waits to be confronted: "I will show you fear in a handful of dust." "I think we are in rat's alley / Where the dead men lost their bones." "I can connect / Nothing with nothing." The pursuit of this pole ultimately leads to a confrontation with divine authority in the form of the Thunder god. Having seen the finitude and nothingness of this world, the speaker finally appears ready to accept meaning from an external source; but his lingering attraction to the world of visionary imagination defeats this movement. The poet's consciousness is finally left in a deadlock between these two opposing forces. Nerval's *El Desdichado* stands as the emblem of the entire *Waste Land*, torn between two separate poetic identities: "*Suis-je Amour ou Phébus? Lusignan ou Biron?*"

• The kind of death represented in the poem's images of emptiness and extreme fragmentation is more horrifying than the womblike death of the drowned Phoenecian sailor. Yet in the final section of the poem, the only one that presents anything like a consistent progression in terms of dramatic action, the

poem's speaker comes close to that crucial apprehension in which
the individual passes from despair to rebirth. Eliot himself
thought that part 5 of *The Waste Land* was "not only the best
part, but the only part that justifies the whole, at all."[32] After
announcing the imminence of death, "We who were living are
now dying," the poem embarks on a journey of denial in which
terms of negation (such as *no, neither, not*) occur twelve times
in the space of twenty-nine lines:

> Here is no water but only rock
> Rock and no water and the sandy road
> The road winding above among the mountains
> Which are mountains of rock without water
> If there were water we should stop and drink
> Amongst the rock one cannot stop or think
>   (331–36)

Apart from the face value of these lines as expressing "the agony
of the lost, parched-throat sensibility,"[33] one discerns in the repeated negation and the obsessive reduplication of single words
a preoccupation with denial that includes an element of self-
torture. The speaker imitates the tantalizing sound of water,
"Drip drop drip drop drop drop," as if willfully intensifying the
effect of its denial. Later poems employ the same language of
repeated negation in the context of a more manifest form of
renunciation:

> Because I cannot drink
> There, where trees flower, and springs flow, for
>   there is nothing again
>   (*Ash-Wednesday*, 1. 14–15)

The first five verse-paragraphs of "What the Thunder Said"
correspond to the "Son of Man" passage in part 1, in the way
they juxtapose interrogation with negation: "Who is the third
who always walks beside you?" "What is that sound high in the
air," "What is the city over the mountains." Heidegger's notion
of *die Seinsfrage* (literally, *the questioning of existence*) sees the
interrogative mood as an initial stage in the search for authenticity. In *The Waste Land*, the speaker's questioning nature at
least distinguishes him, in terms of awareness, from the mindless

"crowds of people," the "hooded hordes swarming." In the original drafts of part 3, a mind "aberrant from the normal equipoise" observes:

> London, the swarming life you kill and breed,
> Huddled between the concrete and the sky,
> Responsive to the momentary need,
> Vibrates unconscious to its formal destiny.[34]

While the interrogative mood upsets the "normal equipoise," images of violence thrust the poem beyond the ensnaring circularity of life in the waste land: "London, your people is bound upon the wheel!"[35] Thus the city that "Cracks and reforms and bursts in the violet light" creates the same effect as the explosive image in *Gerontion* of the characters "whirled / Beyond the circuit of the shuddering Bear / In fractured atoms." In *Gerontion* this disintegration of the symbols of surface reality brings forth visions of lyrical imagination.

The corresponding passage of *The Waste Land* originally followed a similar course, as retreat into the world of pure imagination took the form of simultaneous ascent and descent:

> I saw him creep head downward down a wall
> And upside down in air were towers
> Tolling reminiscent bells—
> And [there were] chanting voices out of cisterns
>   and of wells
>
> . . . .
>
> As a deaf mute swimming deep below the surface
> knowing neither up nor down, swims down and down
> In the calm deep water where no stir nor surf is
> Swims down and down
> And about his hair the seaweed purple and brown.[36]

One sees here a return to the themes of music, stillness, depth, and elevation that characterize passages such as the hyacinth scene and the "Death by Water" section. The final version of the poem, however, neutralizes the original effect of these lines by eliminating the undersea imagery and adding modifiers of darkness and emptiness: a "blackened" wall, "empty" cisterns, "exhausted" wells. The passage as we know it, then, avoids an

escape into the imagination's inner world in order to confront
the face of nothingness. In terms of the existential journey, this
final encounter with nothingness, if really apprehended, can
cause death to lose its terrifying aspect: "Dry bones can harm
no one."

The end of this passage—

> Only a cock stood on the rooftree
> Co co rico co co rico
> In a flash of lightning. Then a damp gust
> Bringing rain

> (392–95)

—suggests the passage from despair to rebirth, the "great reversal," which Helmut Kuhn describes as "a hiatus, total discontinuity, a bursting forth into a hitherto unapproachable reality."[37]
But the remainder of the poem shows that such an interpretation would be premature. To the extent that *The Waste Land*
represents an individual "search for authenticity," the process
is confounded by the survival of imagination in the face of
nothingness.

The invocation of divine authority coincides with this individual search for meaning throughout the poem. The appeal to
the "Son of man," the Buddhist denotation of the Fire Sermon,
the Augustinian prayer at the end of part 3, all reflect at least the
possibility of external sources of order in an intrinsically disordered world. This possibility comes closest to realization in the
dictates of the Upanishad in part 5, where the "divine principle"
repeats a single syllable, *Da*, which the speaker interprets as a
set of moral imperatives: *Datta, Dayadhvam, Damyata* (*give, be
compassionate, restrain yourselves*). The speaker's obsession with
the independent life of the imagination, however, prevents him
from accepting the principles of austere discipline conveyed in
the divine utterance.

In the passage from the Upanishads from which Eliot has
drawn,[38] the Lord of Creation, called Prajapati, speaks to his
threefold offspring—gods, men, and devils—taking each group in
turn:

Having lived the life of a student of sacred knowledge, the gods
said: "Speak to us, sir." To them he spoke this syllable, "Da."

"Did you understand?" "We did understand," said they. "You said to us, 'Restrain yourselves (*damyata*).'" "Yes (*Om*)!" said he. "You did understand."[39]

The process is repeated with the other students in exactly the same way, except that the men understand the syllable as *datta* (give) and the devils as *dayadhvam* (be compassionate). Prajapati commends each group with the same "Yes! you did understand." The brahmana concludes:

This same thing does the divine voice here, thunder, repeat: *Da! Da! Da!* that is, restrain yourselves, give, be compassionate. One should practise this same triad: self-restraint, giving, compassion.

In *The Waste Land* the thunder delivers all three imperatives to men or, more specifically, to the poem's speaker, who responds to each command in a manner at least equivocal, at times evasive. In this particular dialogue of self and soul, the soul is the budding ascetic, the self is the imagination of the natural man, which "confesses its blindness but lives in vision."[40]

To the extent that the Sanskrit words call for exercise of the will in imposing an external order upon experience, the speaker responds by affirming the value of experience with an internal order independent of the will. The answer to the question What have we given? appears to be "nothing" except "The awful daring of a moment's surrender," which is rather a giving *in*.[41] The syntax of the passage associates the moment of surrender with friendship, profound emotion ("blood shaking my heart"), and existence, while it opposes these terms to an age of prudence, to obituaries and empty rooms. The speaker in fact alludes to a moment of privileged being, like the moment in the hyacinth garden, against which the routine of life and death in the waste land becomes "unreal."

To the imperative *Dayadhvam* (be compassionate) the speaker can only attest to the impossibility of compassion in a world where "each confirms a prison." At the same time he affirms the existence of "aethereal rumours" that appear to have less to do with deliberate compassion than with an innate sympathy for the music of Ariel's song and the children singing in the cupola. The final part of this passage alters the original idea of self-restraint to suit one of Eliot's familiar scenes of natural exhilaration, like the sleigh ride in part 1:

> *Damyata*: The boat responded
> Gaily, to the hand expert with sail and oar
> The sea was calm, your heart would have responded
> Gaily, when invited, beating obedient
> To controlling hands
>
> (419–23)

The relationship with nature is one of alliance rather than dominance, so that the directing, sensitive hand, as Kenner points out, becomes "the imagined instrument of a comparably sensitive human relationship."[42]

The vocabulary of this passage removes it from the sexual waste land of the house-agent's clerk, whose "vanity requires no response," and connects it to other passages in which the speaker enters into organic union with an individual or with his natural surroundings. The "beating oars" of the Elizabeth-and-Leicester scene survive in the "sail and oar" and the "beating" heart of this passage, as does the "shaking" heart of momentary surrender. One sees a less direct semantic connection in the sailing image that leads to the hyacinth scene and ultimately to the "heart of light." Of course, the crucial "would have" (added after the original "your heart responded")[43] grammatically relegates this final moment of union to the status of "what might have been," but it does not alter the essential nature of the scene in the speaker's imagination.

In the case of each Sanskrit command then, the speaker's response fails to measure up to what the moral imperative would seem to require. What he has given, if anything, remains unclear; he cannot practice compassion from within the prison of the self; he enlists the idea of control in the service of natural impulses rather than in their suppression. Finally, where the divine imperatives imply the practice of self-discipline in and through time as duration (*chronos*), the Eliotic imagination dwells in "a pattern of timeless moments" (*kairoi*)[44] that intersects with the world of change and decay only in isolated instances: "By this, and this only . . . turn once only . . . Revive for a moment."

The speaking of the thunder dramatizes a conflict, implicit throughout Eliot's work, between a willed form of order and the creative moment, which independent of the will has its own internal order. The unresolved nature of this struggle generates the deliberate confusion of the final eleven lines, where the discordant strains of the poem are brought together in ultimate cacophony. In this respect the form of the final lines stands as a compendium of the poem as a whole. The method of multilingual fragmentation, however, does not prevent one from identifying its separate strains.

The question Shall I at least set my lands in order? sets the speaker apart from the other inhabitants of the waste land in his awareness of death's imminence: "Thus saith the Lord, Set thine house in order: for thou shalt die, and not live" (Isaiah 38:1). In terms of the individual's search for meaning, this acknowledgment of the essential nature of life as "Being-towards-death"[45] is accompanied by the collapse of the structures of day-to-day existence that make it possible to avoid the reality of death. Eliot employs an architectural metaphor for these structures: London Bridge, associated in part 1 with the mindless crowd, is now "falling down." While the individual experiences it as despair, this disintegration of his world can actually prepare him in a purgatorial manner for spiritual rebirth (or, in the existential term, *authenticity*). The line from Dante, *"Poi s'ascose nel foco che gli affina,"* thus focuses on an ascetic theme for which the poem draws on traditions not only Christian, but Buddhist and Hindu as well.

We should know by now that the movement toward asceticism in *The Waste Land* never proceeds very far without interruption. The sudden appearance of the swallow returns us to the theme of creative imagination and its images of flight, elevation, and song. Although Eliot's note to the line urges a comparison with the nightingale in parts 2 and 3, this swallow has more in common with the vision of the hermit-thrush who "sings in the pine trees." The source of Eliot's line in the *Pervigilium Veneris*, written in honor of Venus Genetrix, celebrates the reawakening of nature and the experience of love. The vocative form, "O swallow swallow" offers a parallel with another moment of liberation:

"O City city, I can sometimes hear." Nerval's *Prince d'Aquitaine
à la tour abolie* brings us back to the "Falling towers" of a col-
lapsing world. But it also evokes the dreamlike undersea world of
the drowned sailor—"*J'ai rêvé dans la grotte où nage la sirène*"—
as well as a yearning for the original garden of innocence, "*où le
pampre à la rose s'allie.*"

These echoes from an inviolate inner world, like voices of the
Sirens, undermine the search for meaning in the larger, dissociated universe with which the poem concerns itself. The next
two lines, "These fragments I have shored against my ruins /
Why then Ile fit you. Hieronymo's mad againe," amount to a
statement of artistic purpose in the way they justify the poem's
fragmentary nature as "fitting" to the divergent forces it seeks to
accommodate; but the statement itself does little to reconcile the
inner conflict to which it alludes. The final six words of the poem
reaffirm a submission to external, formal authority in the quest
for order. But these words do not afford deliverance from chaos;
they are uttered in the face of it.

In *The Cocktail Party* (1950) Miss Celia Copleston complains
to her psychiatrist, Sir Henry Harcourt-Reilly, of a condition she
regards as requiring some form of treatment. She tells him:

> I have thought at moments that the ecstasy is real
> Although those who experience it may have no reality.
> For what happened is remembered like a dream
> In which one is exalted by intensity of loving
> In the spirit, a vibration of delight
> Without desire, for desire is fulfilled
> In the delight of living. A state one does not know
> When awake. But what, or whom I loved
> Or what in me was loving, I do not know.
>
> (Act 2)

The psychiatrist sees this condition as leading toward "the final
desolation / Of solitude in the phantasmal world / Of imagination," and he prescribes for his patient a "terrifying journey" that
requires "The kind of faith that issues from despair."

It is symptomatic of the later Eliot that his characters speak of
the creative imagination as a form of disease. More important,

however, the dramatic dialogue reveals a fundamental division in Eliot's poetic sensibility between the experience of imagination as a transcendent order of being and the more sceptical view of it as a cruelly inadequate reaction to the realities of a disordered universe. This division finds its roots in Eliot's earliest work. Poems like *Prufrock* and *Gerontion* soared or plunged into visions of ecstatic fulfillment when faced with the failure of the intellect to establish purpose or even intelligible discourse in an environment of aimless movement and incoherent ritual. Perhaps chastened by its abortive affair with History in *Gerontion*, the intellect relinquishes its role as the active agent of order in *The Waste Land*. When challenged, "What are you thinking of?" the speaker can only reply, "I think we are in rats' alley / Where the dead men lost their bones." Paradoxically, this abdication of the conscious intellect, with its accompanying disintegration of the knowable world, prepares for the recognition of external forms of authority as at least possible sources of order: "O Lord Thou pluckest me out" "Then spoke the thunder." The metaphor of the existential journey provides a model for our understanding of how an awareness of the world as "unreal" can lead to an encounter with nothingness, and ultimately to the unexpected possibility of meaning.

What I have called "imagination" in *The Waste Land* actually refers to a pattern of individual lines and entire passages related by thematic continuity and by parallels in imagery. In this pattern the theme of organic unity (with its recurrent images of depth and sexual fulfillment) combines with the theme of purity (gold, childhood, flight, music, elevation) to form a separate visionary reality secure from the disorder of the waste land. Throughout the poem the attraction to this inner reality of the imagination runs counter to the search for external forms of order and ultimately accounts for the agonized confusion of the poem's ending. Eliot's notes offer as an English equivalent to the last three words of the poem, "The Peace which passeth understanding." But in terms of the divided factions of the poet's sensibility, the peace is but an uneasy cease-fire, and promises renewed hostilities.

NOTES

1. See, for example, A. D. Moody, *Thomas Stearns Eliot: Poet* (Cambridge: At the University Press, 1979), p. 79.

2. T. S. Eliot, "Beyle and Balzac," *Athenaeum*, May 30, 1919.

3. T. S. Eliot, *The Use of Poetry and the Use of Criticism* (London: Faber & Faber, 1964), p. 146.

4. Frye, *Romanticism Reconsidered*, p. 10.

5. [T. S. Eliot,] "Mr. Yeats' Swan Song," *Athenaeum*, April 4, 1919, p. 136. Like most other contributions to this issue, the review is unsigned; but its style and content, as well as the circumstances of its publication, convince me that Eliot is the author. The reader is invited to consider the following points as evidence of Eliot's authorship: (1) Eliot contributed regularly to the weekly *Athenaeum* in 1919, although his initials do not start appearing in the review until the April 25 issue. (2) The references in the Yeats article to Spinoza, Lucretius, Milton, and Blake reflect Eliot's literary interests at the time. (3) Apart from the argument, which conforms to Eliot's general point of view, the style itself is unmistakably Eliot's. He says of Blake, "Like Jacob, he wrestled until the going down of the sun with his angel and would not let him go," and "The phantasmagoria of the dreamer have been mastered by the sheer creative will of the poet." On images in "The Double Vision of Michael Robartes," "These are no more than the dry bones in the valley of Ezekiel, and alas! there is no prophetic metaphor to make them live." And finally, "[Yeats] is by structure and impulse an artist. But structure and impulse are not enough. Passionate apprehension must be added to them."

6. Eliot, "Beyle and Balzac."

7. Cf. Gilbert Durand, *Les Structures anthropologiques de l'imaginaire* (Paris: Presses universitaires de France, 1960), p. 33.

8. D. E. S. Maxwell, *The Poetry of T. S. Eliot* (London: Routledge & Kegan Paul, 1966), p. 103.

9. [Eliot,] "Mr. Yeats' Swan Song."

10. T. S. Eliot, *The Waste Land: A Facsimile and Transcript of the Original Drafts*, ed. Valerie Eliot (New York: Harcourt Brace Jovanovich, 1971), p. 7 (hereafter cited as *TWL, Original Drafts*).

11. See n. 2.

12. Frye, *Romanticism Reconsidered*, p. 17. Cf. Herman Melville, *Moby-Dick*, ch. 87, "But even so, amid the tornadoed Atlantic of my being, do I myself still forever centrally disport in mute calm; and while ponderous planets of unwaning woe revolve around me, deep down and deep inland there I still bathe me in eternal mildness of joy."

13. Eliot, *TWL, Original Drafts*, p. 13.

14. Williamson, *Reader's Guide to T. S. Eliot*, p. 128.

15. Cleanth Brooks, "*The Waste Land*: Critique of the Myth," in Jay Martin, ed., *A Collection of Critical Essays on "The Waste Land"* (Englewood Cliffs, N.J.: Prentice-Hall, 1968), p. 76.

16. The willows drenched, and blossoms on the hedges—
   It is there, in a shower, we took shelter.
   I was seven, she was younger.
   She was completely soaked, I gave her primroses.
   (The translation is my own.)

17. Charles Baudelaire, *Oeuvres complètes* (Paris: Pléiade, 1954), p. 93.

18. Eliot, *TWL, Original Drafts*, p. 123.

19. Quoted in Frye, *Romanticism Reconsidered*, p. 10.

20. Eliot, *Three Voices of Poetry*, p. 21. See ch. 1 of this study.

21. The phrase comes from Virginia Woolf, *Moments of Being* (New York: Harcourt Brace Jovanovich, 1976); see esp. pp. 70–73.

22. William F. Lynch, S.J., *Christ and Apollo: The Dimensions of the Literary Imagination* (New York: Sheed & Ward, 1960), p. 166.

23. *Tristan und Isolde*, I. i: "*Stimme eines jungen Seemannes (aus der Höhe wie vom Maste her, vernehmbar)*."

24. Eliot, *TWL, Original Drafts*, p. 63.

25. Brooks, "*The Waste Land*," p. 74.

26. Eliot, *TWL, Original Drafts*, p. 47.

27. William V. Spanos, " 'Wanna Go Home, Baby?': *Sweeney Agonistes* as Drama of the Absurd," *PMLA* 85 (1970): 8–20.

28. Karl Jaspers, *Way to Wisdom: An Introduction to Philosophy*, trans. Ralph Mannheim (New Haven, Conn.: Yale University Press, 1954), pp. 19–20.

29. Spanos, " 'Wanna Go Home, Baby?' " p. 16.

30. St. John of the Cross, *The Dark Night of the Soul*, trans. and ed. Kurt F. Reinhardt (New York: Ungar, 1957), p. 26.

31. See n. 1.

32. Eliot, *TWL, Original Drafts*, p. 129. Letter to Bertrand Russell, Oct. 15, 1923.

33. M. L. Rosenthal, *The Modern Poets: A Critical Introduction* (London: Oxford University Press, 1965), p. 94.

34. Eliot, *TWL, Original Drafts*, p. 43.

35. Ibid.

36. Ibid., pp. 113, 115.

37. Helmut Kuhn, *Encounter with Nothingness: An Essay on Existentialism* (London: Methuen, 1951), p. 104. Cited in Spanos, " 'Wanna Go Home, Baby?' " p. 9.

38. *Brihad-Aranyaka Upanishad*, 5.2. Eliot's note incorrectly cites 5.1.

39. Robert Ernest Hume, trans., *The Thirteen Principal Upanishads* (London: Oxford University Press, 1949), p. 150.

40. Harold Bloom, *Yeats* (London: Oxford University Press, 1972), p. 375.

41. William Harmon, "T. S. Eliot's Raids on the Inarticulate," *PMLA* 91 (1976) : 454.

42. Kenner, *The Invisible Poet*, p. 177.

43. Eliot, *TWL, Original Drafts*, p. 79.

44. The two kinds of time are discussed in Bornstein, *Transformations of Romanticism*, p. 159.

45. Martin Heidegger, *Being and Time*, trans. John Macquarrie and Edward Robinson (New York: Harper & Row, 1962), p. 296.

CHAPTER THREE

Two Mystical Attitudes

In 1927, the year of his confirmation in the Church of England, Eliot published an essay in French that distinguishes between two kinds of "mystical attitude" in poetry. One such attitude, characteristic of the high medieval age and embodied in the work of Dante, is intellectual and contemplative, requiring *"la sublimation et la subordination de l'émotion et du sentiment dans la vision de Dieu."*[1] Eliot contrasts this attitude with what he sees in Donne and the metaphysical poets as the search for rare moments of ecstatic union in which the poet's soul seems to "dissolve itself" into another soul. Dante's "amour-contemplation" treats the love of Beatrice as a means of apprehending an absolute Good, while Donne's ecstatic union never transcends the human and transitory. *"Prisonnier de ses sentiments,"* the metaphysical poet seeks permanence in the "fixation" of the ephemeral. Dante, on the other hand, devotes himself to *"la recherche, dans l'univers, d'un ordre et d'un sens."*

Six years earlier a more famous essay of Eliot's had praised Donne's "direct sensuous apprehension of thought, or a recreation of thought into feeling."[2] The subsequent devaluation of Donne's poetry in Eliot's esteem reveals the extent to which Eliot's growing religious convictions influenced his critical judgment. More important, the divergent "mystical attitudes" Eliot identifies in Dante and Donne correspond to conflicting values in his own poetry and suggest a way of understanding his poetic development in the years leading up to and immediately following his religious conversion. In the earlier work the conscious quest for an enduring order is continually sabotaged by bursts of visionary experience that occur independently of the mind and will. This fundamental conflict carries forward into the poems of 1925–30, where a form of spirituality based on "the sublimation and subordination of emotion and feeling by the intellect" struggles to contain a poetic imagination drawn to its dreamlike visions of unity and fulfillment. In terms of the peculiar way he defines their two forms of mysticism, Eliot is the type of Donne striving to emulate the example of Dante.

In this middle period of his poetic development Eliot embraces Christianity as an objective structure to satisfy his need for intellectual order—the kind of knowledge that understands experience in conceptual terms. "That is the advantage of a coherent traditional system of dogma and morals like the Catholic," he wrote in a 1929 essay on Dante; "it stands apart, for understanding and assent even without belief, from the single individual who propounds it."[3] Just as Christian dogma offered Eliot a system to which a troubled mind could give rational assent, Christian literary tradition provided a symbolic and thematic framework to oppose his profound sense of disorder. Eliot's liberal use of Dantescan imagery in this period points to a preoccupation with the one poet who saw the universe as a divinely ordered mathematical structure. Hence the search for an ordered poetic world emerges from the virtual paralysis of The Hollow Men to the traditional forms in Ash-Wednesday of askesis, ascent by stages, and contemplation of the divine as personified in the Lady.

While these thematic structures form one alternative to disorder, an equally compelling alternative arises out of the poet's attraction to "ecstatic union" with nature through the synthetic power of imagination. Behind the rhetoric of denial in The Hollow Men lies an imagery of light, elevation, music, and sexuality that survives as a remnant of The Waste Land's inner world of oneiric harmony. Ash-Wednesday expands upon this imagery and develops it into a Romantic vision of interaction between self and nature, while at the same time the poem opposes this vision to a symbolic structure motivated by religious concepts.

The movement from The Hollow Men through Ash-Wednesday, then, has its parallels with the movements leading up to The Waste Land: like Prufrock and Gerontion, Eliot's later poems seek formal and thematic strategies to contain or subdue the Romantic visionary experience. In this respect the voices of the living dead in *The Hollow Men* and of devotion in *Ash-Wednesday* share the function of the ironic persona in the earlier dramatic monologues: each voice protects the poet from the seductive forces of his own "dream kingdom." On a stylistic level, the stark and repetitive quality of language in *The Hollow Men* counteracts an underlying lyricism, while *Ash-Wednesday* wavers between a figurative, metaphorical style motivated by religious belief and a Romantic use of language that unites tenor and vehicle, subject and object. Eliot revives the techniques of Shelley, Wordsworth, and Baudelaire in fusing the poet's sense of personal identity with natural imagery. This "mystical attitude" of spiritual fulfillment in the privileged moment dominates the poet's vision of order in *Marina* and ultimately in the *Four Quartets*.

1

The Hollow Men (published 1925) portrays a poetic consciousness in which intense nostalgia for a state of Edenic purity conflicts with the paradoxical search for a more enduring form of order through acts of denial and alienation. To the common observation that *The Hollow Men* expresses the depths of Eliot's despair, one must add that the poet in a sense *chooses* despair as the only acceptable alternative to the inauthentic existence of the unthinking inhabitants of the waste land. Eliot himself saw this kind of metaphysical despair as more intellectual than emotional. He says of Pascal, a "Christian thinker" with whom he clearly identifies:

> His despair, his disillusion, are . . . no illustration of personal weakness; they are perfectly objective, because they are essential moments in the progress of the intellectual soul; and for the type of Pascal they are the analogue of the.drought, the dark night, which is an essential stage in the progress of the Christian mystic.[4]

Principles of intellectual order control the despair of *The Hollow Men* as well, in the way the poem consciously evaluates experience in abstract terms, distinguishes between antithetical states of being, and establishes, both in form and subject matter, the archetype of the Negative Way as an alternative to disorder as well as to the illusory order of visionary experience. The following pages examine formal and thematic elements of the poem as representing the progress of Eliot's own "intellectual soul," and then show this progress as frustrated by the poet's attraction to a visionary imagery.

The Hollow Men replaces the richly chaotic style of *The Waste Land* with an austerity of expression that prepares for the contemplative mode of *Ash-Wednesday*. In what Bergonzi has called "a virtual surrender to the silence," the formal strategy of *The Hollow Men*, like its thematic content, seems designed to demonstrate how effectively the shadow of the inarticulate falls between the conception and the creation of an artistic work. Formal aspects of the poem imitate the characteristics of the hollow men it portrays. For example, their desire to "avoid speech" finds a counterpart in the poem's general paucity of utterance: the technique of constant repetition and negation—"The eyes are not here / There are no eyes here"—manages to employ only about 180 *different* words in a work 420 words long. The "Paralysed force, gesture without motion" applies not only to the men themselves but also to the poem as a whole, which exhibits little narrative progression in the conventional sense and eschews verbs of direct action.

As the hollow men grope together, form prayers to broken stone, and whisper meaninglessly, so the poem itself gropes toward a conclusion only to end in hollow abstraction, broken prayer, and the meaningless circularity of a child's rhyme. The conscious reduction of poetic expression to a bare minimum does away with metaphor and simile and produces a final section of the poem almost completely devoid of modifiers. The poem avoids capitulation to the silence of the inarticulate by relying on a highly structured syntax that tends to order experience in terms of binary opposition: "Shape without form, shade without colour," or "Between the idea / And the reality / Between the motion / And the act."

The quality of a poetic style marked by verbal austerity and relentless negation forms a structural counterpart to a thematic strategy that repudiates the validity of human experience at every level. In this respect the poem expands upon the theme of denial explored as part of the individual's search for meaning in *The Waste Land*. In modern existential terms as well as those of traditional Christianity, the Negative Way leads ultimately to an encounter with nothingness which, paradoxically, can inspire the individual with faith in God. Kierkegaard seeks to explain this paradox by showing that dread [*aengste*], the simultaneous fear and intense awareness of nothingness, opens up the possibility of faith in an infinite beyond human life by "laying bare all finite aims and discovering their deceptions," by revealing the "dead-endedness" of life itself: "When the discoveries of possibility are honestly administered, possibility will then disclose all finitudes and idealize them in the form of infinity in the individual who is overwhelmed by dread, until in turn he is victorious by the anticipation of faith."[5] The *via negativa* brings the individual to a terminal point marking the boundary between the finite and the infinite.

The Hollow Men explores this boundary situation in its images of finality or extremity and in a thematic structure comprising two different states of being. The poem's speaker anticipates with dread "that final meeting"; the men grope together "In this last of meeting places"; the final section, in its generalized abstraction of all that has gone before, tells us that "This is the way the world ends." The Dantescan image of the lost souls "Gathered on this beach of the tumid river" belongs to a boundary motif that recurs throughout Eliot's poetry: Prufrock escapes from the world of skirts and teacups to the world of visionary imagination via a "walk upon the beach." The protagonist of *The Waste Land* sits down and weeps "By the waters of Leman," then upon the shore "with the arid plain behind me." The sea of *The Dry Salvages* "is the land's edge also." The persona of *The Hollow Men* has arrived, intellectually and imagistically, at the outer limit of one world only to find that its "deliberate disguises" conceal a finite lack of possibility: between the potency and existence "Falls the Shadow."

Order and possibility, if they exist at all, lie outside the dream kingdom of human experience, in a state of being defined only

as "other" and represented in terms of a purely traditional iconography: eyes, perpetual star, multifoliate rose. This latter order
is "The hope only / Of empty men," i.e., of those who, unlike
the *hollow* men, have purged themselves of all disguises to confront the nothingness of their own being.[6] Eliot later describes
this ascetic emptiness more fully as a condition for spiritual
rebirth:

> Internal darkness, deprivation
> And destitution of all property,
> Dessication of the world of sense,
> Evacuation of the world of fancy,
> Inoperancy of the world of spirit;
> This is the one way, and the other
> Is the same. . . .
>   (*Burnt Norton*, 3. 117–23)

Eliot's obsession with the themes of dessication, evacuation, and
inoperancy in *The Hollow Men* comes at a turning point in his
artistic and intellectual development. Artistically, he has abjured
the tragic-heroic style of *The Waste Land* ("These fragments I
have shored against my ruins"), but his particular *"alchimie de
la douleur"* has distilled that poem's admixture of disorder into
a refined essence of despair that *Ash-Wednesday* will transub-
stantiate into the material of devotional verse. Intellectually,
analogues of the drought and the dark night in *The Hollow Men*
represent "an essential stage in the progress of the Christian mystic" as they prepare for the pilgrimage of the later poems.

The *Waste Land* portrayed a presiding consciousness torn between askesis and visionary imagination in its search for a way
out of chaos. The starkness of *The Hollow Men* in turn nearly
obliterates the inner world of unity and fulfillment on which
Eliot has so often relied for his poetic inspiration. But enough
remnants of that world remain to create a substantial ambiguity
of values in this poem. In part 3, for example, the inhabitants of
the "dead land," for all their hollowness, are "Trembling with
tenderness" with "Lips that would kiss." The image recalls the
"blood shaking my heart" of the privileged moment evoked in
the final section of *The Waste Land*, as well as "The notion of
some infinitely gentle / Infinitely suffering thing" in the *Preludes*. As another poem asks, are these ideas right or wrong? The

persona of *The Hollow Men* appears torn between nostalgia for some sort of ecstatic union and the cold-eyed vision of nothingness that alone can lead him to "Death's other kingdom."

The Waste Land combined images of light, elevation, and celestial music in its vision of a pure state of being removed from an unreal quotidian existence. *The Hollow Men* uses similar imagery in describing the eyes perceived in "death's dream kingdom," the illusory realm of the hollow men:

> There, the eyes are
> Sunlight on a broken column
> There, is a tree swinging
> And voices are
> In the wind's singing
> More distant and more solemn
> Than a fading star.
>
> (22–28)

"Death romantically gilded," remarks one commentator.[7] The lines, however, offer a brief reprieve from the language of negation and renunciation that characterizes most of the poem. The images affirm their own value in the speaker's imagination, although the context of the poem as a whole treats this vision as less valid than the potential reappearance of the eyes "As the perpetual star / multifoliate rose." Section 2 incorporates the central problem of the poem and of Eliot's work in general as one where the imagination creates a "dream-vision" of purity, which the intellect rejects in favor of an order that originates outside the self. Here, as elsewhere, the poet finds "fittest for renunciation" that which most attracts him.

Eliot apparently considered for inclusion in *The Hollow Men* a series of shorter poems published in various places from 1922 to 1925.[8] These poems expand upon the poet's problematic relation to the vision of "death's dream kingdom" and suggest that the desolation of *The Hollow Men* expresses a fall from a state of Edenic purity or a loss of ecstatic union with another being. *Eyes that last I saw in tears* (*Chapbook*, 39, 1924) contains these lines:

> Here in death's dream kingdom
> The golden vision reappears

> I see the eyes but not the tears
> This is my affliction

Song to the Opherian (*Tyro*, 1922) contemplates "The golden foot I may not kiss or clutch." The poet's inability to recapture his "golden vision" leads him to question its reality as well as the nature of his own response. He asks in "The wind sprang up at four o'clock" (printed in the 1924 *Chapbook* as one of "Doris's Dream Songs," along with *Eyes that last I saw in tears* and part 3 of *The Hollow Men*):

> Is it a dream or something else
> When the surface of the blackened river
> Is a face that sweats with tears?

The image returns one to the "tumid river" in part 4 of *The Hollow Men*, where hope lies only for those who have emptied themselves of dreams. The poet must renounce his inner Eden or Xanadu in the name of a more lasting salvation. But as the final section of *The Hollow Men* shows with its concern for creation, emotion, response, and desire, the poet still owes allegiance to imagination and ecstatic fulfillment.

Even Eliot's use of Dantescan material in this poem points to a division in his poetic consciousness; he borrows images from Dante's Earthly and Celestial Paradises as if they were diametrically opposed states of being instead of intermediate and final stages on the way to beatitude. The first stanza of part 2 in *The Hollow Men*, for example, conforms to Dante's description of the Earthly Paradise in the final cantos of the *Purgatorio*. In Canto 28 (1–21), on a morning full of sunlight, the tree boughs flutter in a gentle wind that accompanies the birds in their singing. In the next canto (29. 21–23) a "sweet melody" runs through the "shining air" to herald the arrival of Beatrice. As Beatrice tells Dante,

> *Quelli ch'anticamente poetaro*
> *l'età dell'oro e suo stato felice,*
> *forse in Parnaso esto loco sognaro.*
> *Qui fu innocente l'umana radice;*
> *qui primavera sempre ed ogni frutto;*
> *nettare è questo di che ciascun dice.*
> (*Purgatorio* 28. 139–44)

("Those who in ancient times sang of
the age of gold and of its happy state
perhaps on Parnassus dreamed of this
place. Here the human root was inno-
cent, here eternal spring and every
fruit, this is the nectar of which each
tells." The translation is mine.)

While Eliot's dream kingdom derives its imagery partly from
Dante's Eden, his antithetical kingdom of hope in part 4 refers
even more directly to Dante's Heavenly Paradise. The Virgin
Mary appears in *Paradiso* 23 as the single "living star" (*viva
stella*) of which Beatrice says, "*Quivi è la rosa in che il verbo
divino carne si fece*" (There is the rose in which the divine word
was made flesh). In the final stage of his journey, of course,
Dante sees the Elect of Heaven seated on the petals of a multi-
tiered rose (*Paradiso* 30–32). I make these comparisons not to
demonstrate once again Eliot's indebtedness to Dante, but to
point out a crucial difference between the modern poet and his
medieval ancestor. Dante's Earthly Paradise stands, in terms both
of its spatial position and its allegorical meaning, as a stage to
which the soul must rise in its quest for salvation. From here the
soul flies directly to its place in heaven. Eliot's own Eden, on the
contrary, pulls the imagination in the opposite direction. Its
golden vision ultimately deceives, and turns the garden of innocence into a "valley of dying stars." The Eliotic persona must
renounce his vision because he cannot hope to recapture its original purity.

2

As a stage in Eliot's poetic evolution *The Hollow Men* presents
a thematic and stylistic impasse: the arrival at the boundary of
existence offers no further terrain to explore, while any greater
curtailment of poetic expression would lead to a *reductio ad
silentium*. From such a position the poet can hope to further his
art in only two ways: either by embracing an external structure
of symbols or by reestablishing the power of the creative imagination. In *Ash-Wednesday* (published 1930)⁹ Eliot does both. The
aspect of the poet's sensibility that in earlier poems sought to

impose an intellectual order on experience now seeks to construct
an ordered vision out of symbols adapted from Christian tradition: the Lady, the ascending stair, the Rose, the dry bones in
the valley of Ezekiel. The poem uses these symbols in such a way
that they become part of an ascetic and contemplative movement, not wholly traditional in itself, toward a spiritual center of
being: the "silent Word" around which the "unstilled world"
still whirls.

While this structure forms one alternative to the chaos of the
poet's universe, it encounters opposition in a form of order arising from the speaker's fusion with his natural surroundings. This
kind of order underlies Prufrock's identification with the sea-girls
riding seaward, as well as *The Waste Land*'s image of the boat
responding gaily; in fact, it motivates Eliot's perpetual preoccupation with what he calls "ecstatic union" in his criticism of
Donne. *Ash-Wednesday* associates this "order of imagination"
with heart and spirit rather than mind and will, and denotes it in
an imagery of flight, expansion, and correspondence with nature.
The poem opposes a purity of "Unbroken wings" to that of "the
silent sister veiled in white and blue": one image acts as a metaphor for the unifying power of a liberated imagination; the other
stands as an object of contemplation for a mind that fears this
power. These conflicting values may be represented in the following pairs of terms derived from the language and imagery of
the poem; the left-hand column descends from the poet's quest
for intellectual order, while the right-hand column corresponds
to the order created by an independent imagination:

mind	heart
will	spirit
concentration	expansion
contemplation	correspondence
construction	creation

The following analysis of *Ash-Wednesday* explores ways in
which the tension between these two poles of Eliot's sensibility
affects the form of the poem. This approach will finally arrive at
a crucial paradox in that even the poem's conscious quest for
spiritual salvation appears motivated by an underlying attraction

to the inner world of the private imagination; the basic impulse of Eliot's later poems still lies in the characteristically Romantic attempt to recapture a lost state of undissociated being. We shall see that Christianity offers Eliot not only "a structure from without to combat the chaos within,"[10] but also an acceptable context for his visions of purity, and that *Ash-Wednesday* begins a process in which the poet strives to turn his private inner Xanadu into a Christian *Paradiso*.

My reading of *Ash-Wednesday* in general departs from the critical convention of narrative sequence that requires each part of the poem to follow logically, in terms of *fabula* or story, upon the preceding section. According to this tradition *Ash-Wednesday* records a "progress of the soul" in the manner of Dante, St. John of the Cross, and St. Bonaventure. E. E. Duncan Jones proposes the following account of the poem's narrative coherence:

> The sequence begins with a poem of which the centre is the renunciation of a "blessed face" and voice; this is followed by a vision of spiritual renewal, presided over by a Beatrice-figure who is also the Church, as Beatrice was also Theology; then there comes the ascent of a spiritual stair, with a backward glance at carnal loveliness; and then a scene in a garden or churchyard where "she" appears, transfigured and glorified.[11]

Such an interpretation tends to minimize the inner conflicts of the speaker in the interests of tracing his moral and spiritual advancement. It reasons, for example, that since the speaker of part 3 has already experienced the blessed vision of part 2, the images of devouring jaws and "carnal loveliness" can only represent remembered weaknesses of the past that he has already transcended. Derek Traversi places himself firmly in the critical tradition as he writes, "Meanwhile, at all events, they are 'fading' temptations, losing actuality in the present, unable finally to affirm themselves in a new and different situation."[12]

My own reading treats the poem not as a logical development from beginning to end, but rather as a series of variations on a theme. Eliot originally published the first three sections as separate poems, and in a different order from that which the final version of *Ash-Wednesday* assigns them. Each of the six parts of the poem approaches the problem of order in a different way, but none of them resolves it. The speaker's spiritual position at the end of part 6 remains essentially the same as it was at the beginning of part 1.

In terms of poetic style, *Ash-Wednesday* departs less radically from the earlier works than the newly Christian theme has led most commentators to suppose. Parts 1 and 2, appearing as separate works in 1928 and 1927, respectively, extend the combined technique of negation and repetition that dates from *The Waste Land*. The syntactical formality of *Ash-Wednesday* and even something of its liturgical style have already emerged in *The Hollow Men*; the imperative "Let me be no nearer" prefigures the grammatical form of "Let my cry come unto Thee," while fragments of the Lord's Prayer in the earlier poem anticipate the later poem's more extensive use of the mass.

The denial of validity to human experience in *The Hollow Men* finds a formal counterpart in the austerity of its linguistic expression. *Ash-Wednesday* achieves a similar coincidence of form and content in its highly abstract and metaphorical treatment of the world it renounces. Eliot avoids the fatal attraction to the natural world by treating it in indirect terms. The idea of "There, where trees flower, and springs flow" generalizes nature almost to the point of abstraction, and conveys a sense of the speaker's remoteness from the processes of natural life. "I no longer strive to strive towards such things" enacts a grammatical and typographical distancing between I and things that corresponds to the speaker's effort to impose self-isolation. The moment of privileged being, evoked with such pathos in the final section of *The Waste Land*, is treated here in equivocal, impersonal terms that entail no emotional commitment on the part of the speaker: "The infirm glory of the positive hour," "The one veritable transitory power." The speaker reduces human experience to the intellectual notions of time and place, and characterizes his own striving in that realm with ironic metaphor: "Why should the agèd eagle stretch its wings?"

Such devices denote a poetic language whose imagery and stylistic characteristics arise from a specifically conceptual motivation rather than from some more basic phenomenon of the poet's imagination. This principle applies equally to the allegorical style of part 2, which describes the systematic dissolution of the self as a consequence of the renunciatory act. Here the poet employs a natural imagery that in itself repudiates nature: the impossible "posterity of the desert" and the nonexistent "fruit of the gourd" stand for the ultimate Nothingness toward which askesis tends. The bizarre white leopards that so methodically devour the speaker's organs belong to the same fantastic bestiary as do the jeweled unicorns of part 4. In the leopards, the chirping bones, the white-gowned Lady, and the garden "where all love ends," the poet serves the purpose of intellectual order by constructing a symbolic structure that transcends the vicissitudes of time, place, and nature. By the same token, however, he sacrifices the power and authenticity of a poetic expression rooted in actual experience and the interrelation of subject and object. Despite the frequent use of the first person pronoun and the attention to concrete anatomical detail—

> . . . having fed to satiety
> On my legs my heart my liver and that which
>   had been contained
> In the hollow round of my skull
>
>   (2. 2–4)

—the passage lacks the immediacy of suffering which the real act of self-abnegation would seem to require. To borrow the language of an earlier poem, the tone turns a shade too "light and deft" as the soul leaves the body torn and bruised. Elisabeth Schneider apparently shares this impression. She writes, "no conflict is implied, no effort, no strain, no hint that the self has experienced any difficulty in dissolving his will."[13] For this reason the grotesqueness of the imagery, while perhaps intended to ground the scene in corporeal substance, instead heightens the artificial quality of the vision. Comparison with a poem like Baudelaire's *Un Voyage à Cythère*, in which the poet actually feels the teeth tear into his flesh, reveals the degree to which Eliot's poetic imagination suffers in his conscious strategy of subordinating emotion and sentiment to the intellect for his vision of salvation.

In terms of the structure of the poetic image, this intellectualized distillation of expression, with its accompanying dissolution of the self, coincides throughout the poem with the move-

ment toward a center of stillness and silence. In a series of refine-
ments on Prufrock's impulse to "roll the universe into a ball,"
Eliot's quest for a permanent source of metaphysical order here
acquires spatial form in images of concentration and convergence. In part 1, both air and will contract into something "small
and dry" as the speaker prays for the condition of immobility
that will unite him with his spiritual center: "Teach us to sit
still." The world he repudiates, on the other hand, appears in
images of motion and expansion: wings stretch or *fly*, trees
flower, and springs *flow* in verbs whose common initial spirants
match their common quality of spatial extension. The next section renews the theme of concentration and convergence:

> As I am forgotten
> And would be forgotten, so I would forget
> Thus devoted, concentrated in purpose.
>
> (2. 19–21)

Concentration here refers not only to the mind's focus on the
Lady as object of contemplation, but also to the alchemical sense
of the word as reduction of a substance to its purest form: the
"whiteness of bones" thus approaches the purity of the white
gown.

The idea of endings and conclusions has obsessed Eliot throughout his poetic career. We move from the "butt-ends" of Prufrock's days and ways, past the *Preludes'* "burnt-out ends of
smoky days" to *The Boston Evening Transcript* and La Roche-
foucauld, "If the street were time and he at the end of the
street." Gerontion is driven by the Trades to his end in a sleepy
corner, while *The Hollow Men* vacillate between "that final
meeting" and a conviction that "This is the way the world ends."
Ash-Wednesday seeks to rectify the discontinuity of this finite,
terminal world in its conception of a center toward which all
things converge. The paradoxical nature of Eliot's "Lady of silences" derives from a position of spatial as well as spiritual cen-
trality, like the center of Yeats's Great Wheel, in which opposite
phases are reconciled. In this sense, as well as in the more generally allegorical sense, the Lady lies at the center or end of all
love as both final cause and final conclusion:

> End of the endless
> Journey to no end
> Conclusion of all that
> Is inconclusible
> (2. 39–42)

The idea of convergence toward a center animates the image of part 4, where "the fountain sprang up and the bird sang down"; it conceives the "centre of the silent Word" in part 5; and in part 6 it finally allows the speaker to see his life as "The place of solitude where three dreams cross."

As Eliot's conception of order takes form in the image of joining a central point of stillness and silence, he represents disorder in terms of exclusion or separation from that center. Earlier poems have already made us familiar with the poet's fear of isolation, from Prufrock's self-consciousness to those in *The Waste Land* who "think of the key, each in his prison." In *Ash-Wednesday* the speaker's willful separation from one world in favor of another only intensifies his sense of exclusion from both. The bones of part 2 reach the final Garden in the desert, but the speaker himself can only pray for such a condition. He remains where "The Lady is withdrawn." Similarly, a veil conceals the silent sister of part 4, who stands out of reach, "Behind a garden god." The "White light folded, sheathed about her" affirms her inaccessibility even while it sanctifies her, and recalls *Gerontion*'s word within a word "swaddled with darkness." As the sister conceals herself, so the "vision in the higher dream" also remains "unread."

Critics have traditionally read the last line of this section, a phrase from the *Salve Regina* usually said at the end of the mass, as expressing renewed faith in the immortality offered by the Virgin and the "fruit of Thy womb, Jesus." By leaving the prayer incomplete and ending with "exile," Eliot introduces a disturbing ambiguity: "And after this, our exile?" The prayer that ends part 3 has the same kind of ambiguity. The centurion of Matthew 8:8, later cited as a supreme example of faith, says to Christ, "Lord, I am not worthy that thou shouldst come under my roof: but speak the word only, and my servant shall be healed." Eliot's truncated version—

> Lord, I am not worthy
> Lord, I am not worthy
> but speak the word only.
>   (3. 23–25)

—makes it possible to read the phrase as a simple declarative (with *I* as the subject of *speak*) rather than as a second-person imperative: "I am not worthy, as I only *speak* the word." The speaker's sense of exclusion resurfaces in part 5 with the image of "Children at the gate / Who will not go away and cannot pray," and in the penultimate line of the poem: "Suffer me not to be separated."

The poem's tensions between concentration and expansion, between convergence and separation, translate in part 3 into the opposition of ascent and descent. In earlier poems the image of the stair denotes the reluctant approach toward some sort of confrontation or assignation: Prufrock's desperate impulse to "turn back and descend the stair," the speaker in *Portrait of a Lady* feeling as though he had mounted on his "hands and knees," the grimly determined "Mount" leading to the last twist of the knife in *Rhapsody on a Windy Night*. *Ash-Wednesday*'s Dantescan image of the three stairs provides a numerically ordered structure that conforms to Eliot's tendency to see his spiritual development as a rational process, a quest guided by the intellect in "stops and steps of the mind." This section parallels the tripartite structure of the Upanishadic passage in *The Waste Land*, where allusions to a private inner life alternate with the three successive moral imperatives of the thunder. Here the willful ascent of the speaker is interrupted three times by an irrational attraction downward or away from his intended course. In the initial verse-paragraph he sees "below" the twisted shape of inner disorder. At the next stage he stares, Jonah-like, into the mouth of an abyss:

> There were no more faces and the stair was dark,
> Damp, jaggèd, like an old man's mouth drivelling,
>   beyond repair
> Or the toothed gullet of an agèd shark.[14]
>   (3. 9–11)

Ash-Wednesday, part 3, contains the stuff of nightmares. Gilbert Durand would see here the primordial terror of the unknown in the archetype of the bestial *"gueule dévorante."*[15] Northrop Frye might refer us to the world of the deep interior in Romantic poetry, which holds not only the springs of creation but also the demon of death:[16]

> For know that there are two worlds of life and death;
> One that which thou beholdest; but the other
> Is underneath the grave, where do inhabit
> The shadows of all forms that think and live
> Till death unite them and they part no more;
> Dreams and the light imaginings of men,
> And all that faith creates or love desires,
> Terrible, strange, sublime and beauteous shapes.
> (*Prometheus Unbound* 1. 1. 195–202)

In either case the downward glance reveals an inner reality that lies beyond the control of a rational, ascending mind. The closing passage of part 3 opens a window onto the other face of this deep interior, where inhabit the light imaginings of men and all that love desires:

> And beyond the hawthorn blossom and a pasture scene
> The broadbacked figure drest in blue and green
> Enchanted the maytime with an antique flute.
> Blown hair is sweet, brown hair over the mouth blown,
> Lilac and brown hair;
> Distraction, music of the flute, stops and steps of
>   the mind over the third stair
> (*Ash-Wednesday*, 3. 14–19)

Critics have universally interpreted this passage as the poet's repudiation of sensual pleasure in his spiritual ascent. Few, however, have noted how the outward negation overlies a partial affirmation; as Bergonzi remarks, "the sensibility that can present the scene is certainly not dessicated or bloodless."[17] Despite the explicitly sexual introduction through a "slotted window bellied like the fig's fruit," the passage involves more than mere carnal desire. The speaker enters momentarily into a world of pastoral enchantment, where elements of music, nature, and human beauty merge in a union perceived instinctively rather than conceptually.

Prufrock's sojourn in the chambers of the sea and the hyacinth scene in *The Waste Land* share this same quality of creating a separate harmony amid the poem's surrounding universe of disorder. "Blown hair is sweet, brown hair over the mouth blown" imitates the reverberating cadence of the flute as syntax gives way to pure image, and "lilac and brown hair" lose their discreteness in the speaker's mind. The real danger here lies not in sexual temptation but in a more alluring state of being that challenges the primacy of the intellect or authorial consciousness. In passages such as this one Eliot approaches a Romantic submission of the self to the natural world, an empathic absorption in nature and other beings that threatens the poet with the loss of his identity.[18] In combating the music of the flute with "stops and steps of the mind," the speaker of *Ash-Wednesday* resists the attraction to ecstatic union in favor of the mental quest as an approach to experience that emphasizes distinction, separation, and steady progress toward a fixed goal of order.

Rather than recounting a past struggle that the speaker can now recall from a position of security, this section of the poem enacts an actual conflict between ordered ascent and descent into an inner realm of the mind with its own laws of order and disorder. The use of the past tense does not make this struggle any less immediate than the vision of the Lady in part 4, also rendered in a grammatical past. The "Fading, fading" of part 3, which Traversi and others assign to the poet's temptations could just as easily apply to "mind" and "strength," thus leading to the confession, "Lord, I am not worthy." The speaker's self-condemnation arises from a failure to resolve his inner discord.

The opposition between willed, contemplative order and the involuntary attraction to a state of ecstatic union acquires renewed intensity in the final section of *Ash-Wednesday*:

> (Bless me father) though I do not wish to wish
>   these things
> From the wide window towards the granite shore
> The white sails still fly seaward, seaward flying
> Unbroken wings
>
> And the lost heart stiffens and rejoices
> In the lost lilac and the lost sea voices

And the weak spirit quickens to rebel
For the bent golden-rod and the lost sea smell
Quickens to recover
The cry of quail and the whirling plover
And the blind eye creates
The empty forms between the ivory gates
And smell renews the salt savour of the sandy earth

(6. 7–19)

Once again, commentators have tended to discount the actuality of this opposition by treating the passage as a lapse of nostalgia for the earthly joys in a mind that has already passed to a higher understanding of things. George Williamson even sees the passage as demonstrating the newly acquired strength of the speaker's faith: "The reversal [from part 1] is now complete: where he could turn neither to the world nor to God, now although he can turn to the world he desires to turn to God."[19] This interpretation takes the poem at face value; the poet, after all, dismisses his lyrical vision as "empty forms between the ivory gates." But it also overlooks the way the synthetic power of imagination here rivals or surpasses conscious faith in unifying the fragmented elements of Eliot's poetic universe.[20] The ideals of purity and oneness the poet seeks in his disciplined contemplation of the Lady are in some sense already realized by a momentarily liberated imagination.

Images of expansion and flight in this passage defy earlier attempts at concentration and contraction. The "wide window" enlarges the "slotted window" of part 3 and opens into infinite space—"The white sails still fly seaward, seaward flying"—as the phrase wheels upon its comma to reflect rhetorically the soaring movement of "Unbroken wings" and the "whirling plover." The equation of sails and wings counteracts the assertion of part 1 ("Because these wings are no longer wings to fly") as it establishes common ground with images of fulfillment in the earlier poems: Prufrock's mermaids "riding seaward," Gerontion's "Gull against the wind," and the gaily responding boat of "What the Thunder Said." Apart from the purely visual quality of *Ash-Wednesday*, part 4, much of its lyrical effect arises from extensive use of consonance, alliteration, and vocalic rhyme: "*wide window* . . . *white* . . . *wings*," "*towards* . . . *shore*" "*sails still* . . . *seaward*,

seaward," "stiffens ... quickens." At the same time an incantatory quality emerges from repeated cadences. Four successive
lines, for example, open with two unstressed syllables followed by
two syllables that the stressed:

> And the lost heart ...
> In the lost lilac ...
>
> And the weak spirit ...
> For the bent golden-rod ...
>
> (6. 11–14)

This section's formal aspects of rhythm and rhyme correspond to
its thematic content in displaying a feeling for the musical qualities of language that exceeds other parts of the poem. The word-
play of part 5 seems self-conscious and overemphatic by comparison:

> If the unheard, unspoken
> Word is unspoken, unheard;
> Still is the unspoken word, the Word unheard,
> The Word without a word, the Word within
> The world and for the world. ...
>
> (5. 2–6)

As the dual appeal to "heart" and "spirit" suggests in part 6,
the speaker experiences more than a merely sensual attraction to
the joys of nature. In fact, the passage in question describes an
interaction of subject and nature that links it to Romantic ideas
of order. Among the elements of the Romantic image that distinguish it from the pre-Romantic mode, William K. Wimsatt
cites: (1) the fusion of the natural and the human or of the subject and his landscape; (2) the identity of tenor and vehicle in
poetic expression, or a blurring of literal and figurative language.[21]
These properties mark a qualitative difference between the first
part of Ash-Wednesday, part 6, and, let us say, part 4 of the same
poem. Part 6 establishes a direct but complex interrelation between the elements of nature and the speaker's inner life, his
heart and spirit. The landscape that attracts the speaker exists
objectively, but it also acquires ideal existence and psychological
value in the speaker's imagination as cause for rejoicing, motive
for rebellion, object of creation. By portraying the landscape as

something both inside and outside him, the speaker indirectly acknowledges himself as part of a universal natural order, the "one life within us and abroad."

The pre-Romantic relation between the subject and his landscape generally limited itself to the allegorical, the metaphysical, or the associative; in this respect William Hazlitt reflects the influence of philosophers like Hume and Hartley when he writes, "It is because natural objects have been associated with the sports of our childhood, . . . with our feelings in solitude . . . that we love them as we do ourselves."[22] The Romantics replaced this purely associative relation with one of identity, such that nature now observes man *"avec des regards familiers."* Eliot's poem identifies two words such as *heart* and *lilac* structurally as well as thematically; both occupy the same position in successive lines and follow the same modifier. A similar structural parallel equates *spirit* and *golden-rod*. The presence of "lost sea voices" not only completes a triangular relation with "lost heart" and "lost lilac," but also reinforces the notion of communication or correspondence with nature.

Comparing this passage to part 4, we find that a different kind of order governs the relation between nature and the female figure "Who walked between the violet and the violet" (the first-person *I* of part 3 having for the time being receded into the background as observer or beholder of the vision). Some commentators have noted that Eliot models his lady partly on the nature-goddess of Baudelaire's *"Bohémiens en voyage"*: *"Cybèle, qui les aime, augmente ses verdures, / Fait couler le rocher et fleurir le désert."* The two figures differ, however, in terms of their relation to the landscape. Cybèle symbolizes the animating spirit of nature, not transcending but immanent in and breathing through living things.[23] Eliot's lady, on the other hand, exists apart from nature and acts upon an essentially passive landscape: "Who then made strong the fountains and made fresh the springs / Made cool the dry rock and made firm the sand." She moves "between" the violets rather than in them or through them, restoring order in nature from an external position. The formalized "various ranks of varied green" suggest control over the landscape rather than fusion with it. The natural imagery of part 4 reflects a rational order bestowed from above and conforming to Eliot's conscious

quest for "a spiritual explanation"[24] of the world. Part 6, on the
other hand, offers a vision that corresponds with Coleridge's concept of organic form insofar as its ordering principle arises internally from the spontaneous interaction of subject and object,
what Wordsworth called an "ennobling interchange of action
from within and without."

This fusion of the human and the natural in part 6 coincides
with a merging of the literal and figurative in language. Again we
may compare the clearly figurative part 4, where tenor and vehicle remain distinct: the tenor of this section concerns the poet's
faith in the Christian trinity and the effect of this faith on his
life; the images of the silent sister and the garden provide the
vehicle. The poet repeatedly reminds us of the analogical value
of his language by pointing out, for example, that "blue of lark-
spur" is also "blue of Mary's colour."

The metaphorical structure of part 6 tends to resist this kind
of separation into component terms. If the tenor of the third
verse-paragraph has to do with the speaker's attraction to nature,
then this is not an object distinct from the vehicle. Language
here succeeds in being literal and figurative at the same time. The
white sails flying seaward may stand for the poet's rebellious
spirit, but they also stand for their own pure image; they acquire
literal presence in addition to their metaphorical function. One
cannot say the same of the white leopards in part 2, or the
"desert in the garden the garden in the desert" of part 5.

The qualitative differences between the language of part 6 (or,
at any rate, the eighth through the nineteenth lines of this section) and that of other parts of the poem points to a crucial
divergence in sources of poetic inspiration. Throughout Eliot's
work the imagination periodically bursts forth to create moments
of an intense fulfillment that eludes the more rational and contemplative side of his sensibility. In the case of *Ash-Wednesday*,
the way this order of imagination rivals the order of intellect is
reflected partly in the poet's choice of verbs. In part 6 the eye
"creates" and the heart "rejoices," where the I of part 1 must
"construct something / Upon which to rejoice." Where the lady
of part 4 makes strong, makes firm, makes fresh, and restores,
the substantives of part 6 stiffen, quicken, renew, and recover.
The poet secretly affirms the action of his imagination by describ-

ing it with the kinds of verbs hitherto reserved for the depiction of his mental quest. This underlying affirmation, of course, runs counter to an overt condemnation in terms of the poet's choice of adjectives: *lost* heart, *weak* spirit, *blind* eye, *empty* forms. The presiding logic of the poem must dismiss the imagination with such disclaimers or else surrender the primacy of mind and will.

3

The tension between two alternatives to disorder has characterized Eliot's poetic career from the beginning, but the peculiar intensity of this conflict in *Ash-Wednesday* signals an attempt by a reasoning, ordering intellect to invade the precincts of the imagination's inner world. *The Waste Land* revealed this inner world alternately in terms of depth, stillness, and silence on the one hand, and flight, music, and natural purity on the other. *The Hollow Men* suppressed this world beneath its language of repetition, negation, and denial, thereby approaching a kind of zero-degree of poetic expression. But Eliot could hardly develop any further in this direction without surrendering to total silence, the poetic counterpart of metaphysical nothingness.

Ash-Wednesday inaugurates a new strategy in the war of intellect and imagination: the mind of the poet seeks to domesticate his Romantic inner Xanadu by enlisting its imagery in the service of a Christian ideal. The downward and inward movement of earlier poems toward "the heart of light, the silence" translates into *Ash-Wednesday*'s movements of convergence toward a spiritual center of stillness and silence. The "lady of silences" and her garden of sanctified natural imagery evolves from the hyacinth girl of *The Waste Land*. The image of the scattered bones "Forgetting themselves and each other, united / In the quiet of the desert" now recalls the drowned sailor who "Forgot the cry of gulls . . . A current under sea / Picked his bones in whispers."

This systematic mining of the world of the deep interior and the conversion of its images to symbols of intellectual order reflect a preoccupation with the example of Dante that dates from before *The Waste Land*. As early as 1920 (in *The Sacred Wood*) Eliot defends what he perceives as a "mechanical framework" in the *Divine Comedy*: "As the centre of gravity of emotions is more remote from a single human action, or a system of purely human actions, than in drama or epic, so the framework has to be more artificial and apparently more mechanical."[25] This notion of the source of emotion as a psychological center remote from human action corresponds to the universe of *The Waste Land*, where images of a deep inner life remain secure from the chaotic world of quotidian reality. However, Eliot particularly admires in Dante what he sees as the subjection of this inner life to a structure of intelligible order: "Dante's is the most comprehensive, and the most *ordered* presentation of emotions that has ever been made" (the emphasis is Eliot's).[26]

The problem of order and emotion arises frequently in Eliot's critical essays of the decade leading up to the publication of *Ash-Wednesday*. In a 1929 essay defending the rigors of Christian dogma against the diluting influences of religious humanism, Eliot at age forty-one alludes indirectly to the process of his own conversion: "Rational assent may arrive late, intellectual conviction may come slowly, but they come inevitably without violence to honesty and nature. To put the sentiments in order is a later and immensely difficult task: intellectual freedom is earlier and easier than complete spiritual freedom."[27] *Without violence*— Eliot's very choice of words implies the latent potential for war between protagonists such as "intellectual conviction" and "nature." The passage as a whole, moreover, implies that the more difficult task of putting "the sentiments in order" does not escape this inner violence.

This critical concern for the synthesis of reason and emotion points to the unresolved tensions of Eliot's poetic work. *Ash-Wednesday* constructs a symbolic framework based primarily on rational assent and intellectual conviction at the expense of other sources of inspiration. Such a framework, however, is not comprehensive enough to bring under control the entire range of the poet's creative impulses: the imagination ultimately rebels in its expansive images of flight and union with nature, thereby frustrating the poet's attempt to put his sentiments in order.

The tensions informing *Ash-Wednesday* appear to resolve themselves momentarily in the lyric *Marina* (published September 1930, five months after *Ash-Wednesday*), but only because in this case the poet does not attempt to subject his imagination to external standards of order. On the contrary, *Marina* revives the purely Romantic practice of deriving a spiritual meaning from the fusion of the subject with objects in nature. As Wimsatt points out, this meaning took form imaginatively and without the explicit religious and philosophical statements one finds in pre-Romantic verse[28]—for example in Pope: "Here then we rest: 'The Universal Cause / Acts to one end, but acts by various laws' " (*Essay on Man*, 3. 1-2). Instead the Romantic imagination expressed its theology in terms of a divinity immanent in the universe, but beyond the pale of rational doctrine:

> Hence, in a season of calm weather,
> Though inland far we be,
> Our souls have sight of that immortal sea
> Which brought us hither;
> Can in a moment travel thither—
> And see the children sport upon the shore,
> And hear the mighty waters rolling evermore.
> (Wordsworth, *Intimations of Immortality*, 161–67)

The images that *Ash-Wednesday* condemned as "empty forms between the ivory gates" return in *Marina* to reveal a "grace dissolved in place":

> What seas what shores what grey rocks and what
> islands
> What water lapping the bow
> And scent of pine and the woodthrush singing
> through the fog
> What images return
> O my daughter[29]
>
> (1–5)

Here the speaker unites with natural objects through extensions of the self in the figure of the daughter and the "half conscious" creative act: "I made this, I have forgotten / And remember."

Where *Ash-Wednesday* developed an imagery of convergence and intersection in opposition to movements of flight and extension, *Marina* reintegrates these two faces of the poet's inner world: the imagination's expansion outward over the marine landscape merges thematically with the descent into a subaqueous world of confluences:

> Whispers and small laughter between leaves and
>   hurrying feet
> Under sleep, where all the waters meet.

The poem's only homage to doctrine comes in a kind of catalog of the damned, which the poet perhaps felt necessary to justify his Romantic vision:

> Those who sharpen the tooth of the dog, meaning
> Death
> Those who glitter with the glory of the hummingbird,
>   meaning
> Death
> Those who sit in the sty of contentment, meaning
> Death
> Those who suffer the ecstasy of the animals, meaning
> Death
>
>   (6–13)

The poet's passion for theological order does not here, as in *Ash-Wednesday*, cause him to renounce his vision of ecstatic union with the created world. *Marina* instead reaffirms the inner world of imagination as the poet's primary source of inspiration. The crucial difference between these two poems suggests the presence of a creative imagination that both nourishes faith and rebels against it. The imagination makes faith possible insofar as this faith must embrace the possibilities of the infinite. But it undermines that aspect of religious faith which requires submission to an external system of order. This tension ultimately results in the curious iconography of the *Four Quartets*, where symbols of traditional Christianity disguise an essentially Romantic universe.

NOTES

1. T. S. Eliot, "Deux attitudes mystiques: Dante et Donne," *Chroniques* 3 (1927):149–73 (Roseau d'Or, 14). A translation by Jean de Menasce of one of the unpublished Clark lectures.
2. Eliot, "The Metaphysical Poets" (1921), in *Selected Essays*, p. 241.
3. Eliot, "Dante" (1929), in *Selected Essays*, p. 219.
4. Eliot, "The *Pensées* of Pascal" (1931), in *Selected* Essays, p .364.

See John D. Margolis, *T. S. Eliot's Intellectual Development* (Chicago: University of Chicago Press, 1972), for a discussion of Eliot's conversion to Anglo-Catholicism as an intellectual process.

5. Søren Kierkegaard, *The Concept of Dread*, trans. Walter Lowrie (Princeton: Princeton University Press, 1944), p. 141.

6. Cf. Harold F. Brooks, "Between *The Waste Land* and the First Ariel Poems: 'The Hollow Men,' " *English* 16 (Autumn 1966):93.

7. Ibid., p. 91. Richard Meckel, a student of American and English burial practices, has informed me that the broken column was a popular form of graveyard monument in the nineteenth century and that it most often symbolized a life cut short in youth.

8. Stead, *The New Poetic*, pp. 168–69, provides a coherent account of the poem's development from *Song to the Opherian* to the final version of *The Hollow Men*.

9. The first three sections of the poem were published, with slight variations from their final form, as separate works during the period 1927–29. They appeared in the following order: section 2 in the *Saturday Review of Literature*, December 1927, entitled *Salutation*; section 1 in *Commerce*, Spring 1928, entitled *Perch'io non spero*; and section 3 in *Commerce*, Autumn 1929, entitled *Som de l'escalina*. The remaining sections were published for the first time in April 1930 as part of the complete poem.

10. Bornstein, *Transformations of Romanticism*, p. 150.

11. E. E. Duncan Jones, "Ash-Wednesday," in Balachandra Rajan, ed., *T. S. Eliot: A Study of His Writings by Several Hands* (1947; reprint ed., New York: Russell & Russell, 1966), pp. 37–38.

12. Derek Traversi, *T. S. Eliot: The Longer Poems* (New York: Harcourt Brace Jovanovich, 1976), p. 72.

13. Elisabeth Schneider, *T. S. Eliot*, p. 115.

14. This amplifies the horror of an image in the prose poem *Hysteria* (published 1917), in which comic situation spreads a thin disguise over the danger of psychological derangement: "I was drawn in by short gasps, inhaled at each momentary recovery, lost finally in the dark caverns of her throat, bruised by the ripple of unseen muscles." In a manner later to prove central to Eliot's sensibility, the conclusion of this minor piece enlists the powers of will and concentration against the forces of hysteria: "I decided that if the shaking of her breasts could be stopped, some of the fragments of the afternoon might be collected, and I concentrated my attention with careful subtlety to this end."

15. Gilbert Durand, *Les Structures anthropologiques de l'imaginaire* (Grenoble: Presses universitaires de France, 1960), pp. 79–86.

16. Frye, "The Drunken Boat," in *Romanticism Reconsidered*, p. 19.

17. Bergonzi, *T. S. Eliot*, p. 140.

18. Cf. Frederick Garber, "Nature and the Romantic Mind," *Comparative Literature* 29 (Summer 1977):206.

19. Williamson, *Reader's Guide to T. S. Eliot*, p. 184.

20. Bornstein is one of the few commentators who appears to recognize this rivalry: "Having extinguished his own will to find peace in God's, the poet discovers that nature threatens to revive it by double appeal to his emotions ("heart") and spirit" (*Transformations of Romanticism*, p. 151).

21. William K. Wimsatt, Jr., "The Structure of Romantic Nature Imagery," in Harold Bloom, ed., *Romanticism and Consciousness* (New York: Norton & Co., 1970), pp. 77–88. See n. 13.

22. William Hazlitt, "On the Love of the Country," in *The Round Table* (1817; reprint ed., London: Bell & Daldy, 1871), p. 26.

23. The terminology is Wimsatt's. "Romantic Nature Imagery," p. 83.

24. Eliot, "The *Pensées* of Pascal," in *Selected Essays*, p. 360.

25. T. S. Eliot, *The Sacred Wood* (1920; reprint ed., London: Methuen, 1972), p. 167.

26. Ibid., 168.

27. Eliot, "Second Thoughts about Humanism" (1929), in *Selected Essays*, p. 438.

28. Wimsatt, "Romantic Nature Imagery," p. 83.

29. Compare the identification of Baudelaire's "daughter, sister" with the landscape in *L'Invitation au voyage*:

> Mon enfant, ma soeur,
> Songe à la douceur
> D'aller là-bas vivre ensemble!
> Aimer à loisir
> Aimer et mourir
> Au pays qui te ressemble!

CHAPTER FOUR

The Disjunctive Universe of Four Quartets

A LETTER from Eliot to Stephen Spender dated March 1931 responds to a query concerning the late string quartets of Beethoven:

> I have the A Minor Quartet on the gramophone, and find it quite inexhaustible to study. There is a sort of heavenly or at least more than human gaiety about some of his later things which one imagines might come to oneself as the fruit of reconciliation and relief after immense suffering; I should like to get something of that into verse before I die.[1]

Like many of Eliot's personal and critical statements, these lines suggest a direct connection between the motive for poetic composition and the poet's desire for a resolution of his inner torment. As several critical studies have demonstrated, the *Four Quartets* can be treated primarily as an affirmation of religious experience or as a "search for eternal reality."[2] But the very nature of such approaches ignores the dimension of conscious and unconscious psychological motivation in the poetic act. Using Durand's theory of the psychological structure of the imagination, Michel Benamou writes that the motivation for poetic expression actually lies in the creation of the self: "By his images, by the new forms which he invents, he accomplishes a self-creation, at times a self-cure. This is what Wallace Stevens means when he says: 'Poetry is a cure of the mind.' "[3] In terms of this phenomenology of the poetic act, the *Four Quartets* represent Eliot's final attempt at creating a unified self out of the opposing faces of his poetic identity.

As a structural model for each of these poems, Eliot chose the form he and Pound had arrived at rather fortuitously in the final version of *The Waste Land*, so that the aleatory qualities of the earlier poem became reified as a pattern which Eliot would impose on his later poetic material. Each of the quartets follows *The Waste Land*'s five-part division: the treatment of visionary experience in part 1; the shift to more discursive passages in parts 2 and 3 with corresponding changes in scene; the single, tightly written lyric of part 4, and the outward thematic expansion of the final section. Helen Gardner's publication of the original drafts to the quartets makes clear, however, that their composition was a highly controlled process in comparison with the radical metamorphoses of the earlier poem.

In contrast to the relatively spontaneous and undirected way in which the raw material of *The Waste Land* emerged, the *Four Quartets* were apparently conceived according to preliminary schemes that followed the outline of rational argument. Thus the scheme for *The Dry Salvages*, for example, ran as follows in Eliot's notes:

1. Sea picture—general
2.   —particular
                       problem of permanence
                       of past pain
3. Past error can only be reconciled
   in eternity. Arjuna & Krishna.
4. Invocation to the B.V.M.
   meaning of "mother" & "father."
5. *Generalisation*: Liberation from
   the past is liberation from the
   future. To get beyond time &
   at the same time deeper into
   time. The Spirit & the Earth.[4]

In their association of "Sea picture" with past pain and error, these lines recall the poet's struggle at the end of *Ash-Wednesday* with the siren songs of nature: the "lost sea voices" he must banish to hear the voice of the Word. At the same time, such a scheme suggests an original motive for composition: Eliot wanted to write a poem that would subdue the unwieldy material of his visionary imagination within the confines of a sequentially ordered rational construct, moving carefully from the general to the particular and back again. The search for an eternal reality that traditional thematic explication commonly attributes to the *Four Quartets* can thus be seen as merely the surface manifestation of another search: for a cease-fire or negotiated settlement between the warring impulses of Eliot's poetic energies. The "liberation" from past and future that Eliot ultimately looks for in the realm "beyond time" is really liberation from a poetic state of siege.

Ash-Wednesday gave form to a poetic persona torn between imagination's fulfillment in the created world and the mind's need for a more permanent, external source of understanding: "Our peace in His will." The *Four Quartets* achieve a partial resolution of this conflict by placing the imagination's moments of visionary experience at the center of a metaphysically conceived universe. As if finally recognizing that his "lost heart" and "weak spirit" actually achieved the sense of unity he sought more consciously in "stops and steps of the mind," the poet of the *Four Quartets* makes the enchanting vision into the object of his mental quest rather than something that distracts it.

The *Four Quartets* fall short of a final reintegration of intellect and imagination, however, because of a complex division in their thematic and stylistic structure. In each of these poems the language of the visionary imagination, with its fusion of self and nature, separates itself on a formal level from the poet's attempt to justify his vision in conceptual terms. But this conceptually motivated language divides itself in turn between an orthodox Christian endeavor to relate the visionary experience to historical or quotidian reality and a mystical attempt to escape from a world bound by time and space. These tensions among different kinds of language point to a curious double split in Eliot's poetic consciousness, a sort of fault system in the psychological terrain of the poem; the disjuncture between visionary experience and the intellect adjoins another break between divergent aims of the intellect. These discontinuities in the poet's mind account for the various stylistic shifts in the poem, where a characteristically Romantic use of language and imagery contrasts either with an abstract discursive language or with a self-consciously allegorical style.

What I consider characteristically Romantic in Eliot's poetic practice involves, on a stylistic level, the merging of tenor and vehicle, the surrender of the speaker's authorial consciousness to natural forces, and the identification of the outer landscape with the speaker's inner world of dream or imaginative vision. In terms of imagery, this kind of language typically entails a dispersion of the elements of self (mind, heart, soul) and their fusion or interaction with natural elements, the endowment of landscape with human or divine qualities, and the development of a series of correspondences among the elements of that landscape.[5] In isolating this phenomenon in Eliot's work, I wish to distinguish it from other senses in which Eliot has been called Romantic or Symbolist: these refer to narrative structure, adaptation of mythology, and internalization of quest patterns in his poems, as well as his views on the emotive origin, social function, and historical evolution of poetry.[6] The point is not to make a Romantic out of Eliot, but to identify a particular kind of natural vision in his work that even at this late stage of his career runs counter to his need to organize reality in terms of intellectual constructs.

Each of the *Four Quartets*, then, comprises just such a natural vision and the various attempts of the poet's mind to attach a conceptual and moral significance to the vision. These two kinds of mental action operate separately in the poem rather than in some form of creative fusion, thus creating tension between two rival sources of poetic inspiration. As the poet is forced to devise means of approaching discursively what his visionary imagination creates intuitively, the idea of language itself as the primary weapon of the intellect comes under increasing attack. Eliot ultimately arrives at an artistically suicidal position that sees the poetic ideal as beyond thought and language, in fact, beyond poetry itself: "The poetry does not matter." With the last of the *Four Quartets* Eliot abandons poetry as the broken-down vehicle of his fight to recover a vision of unity that "has been lost / And found and lost again and again."

This chapter takes the *Four Quartets* one by one, in each case focusing on a detailed analysis of the visionary experience embodied in the first section of the poem. It then selects representative passages from the remainder of the poem that struggle to adapt the vision to a scheme of intellectual order. These passages use allegory and conceptual abstraction to attach a doctrinal value to the vision, or else they consign it to the lower levels of Eliot's metaphysical hierarchy through techniques of repetition and enumeration: "To explore the womb, or tomb, or dreams; all these are usual / Pastimes and drugs, and features of the press." As a corollary to this problem of relating visionary experience to conceptual knowledge, my reading follows the theme of language through all of the poems, to where the limitations of language itself stand for the irreconcilable division of the poet's identity.

1

In *Burnt Norton* (published 1936) the vision of the rose garden in part 1 defies later attempts to approximate it in purely abstract terms, as well as counterattempts at integrating the vision with a time-governed world. This difficulty in assimilation points to the problem of reconciling two qualitatively different kinds of poetic experience: the visionary absorption of the self in nature or other selves, and the antithetical reassertion of authorial consciousness that sees the world as conforming to intellectual constructs. Simple stylistic analysis suffices to counterdistinguish these two kinds of experience in *Burnt Norton*. In the rose garden passage, the relation of subject and landscape, fusion of tenor and vehicle, particularity of setting, and spatial and semantic quality of imagery all characterize what we defined in earlier poems as the manifestation of Eliot's visionary imagination:

> Footfalls echo in the memory
> Down the passage which we did not take
> Towards the door we never opened
> Into the rose-garden. My words echo
> Thus, in your mind.
>   But to what purpose
> Disturbing the dust on a bowl of rose-leaves
> I do not know.
>   Other echoes
> Inhabit the garden. Shall we follow?
> Quick, said the bird, find them, find them,
> Round the corner. Through the first gate,

Into our first world, shall we follow
The deception of the thrush? Into our first world.
There they were, dignified, invisible,
Moving without pressure, over the dead leaves,
In the autumn heat, through the vibrant air,
And the bird called, in response to
The unheard music hidden in the shrubbery,
And the unseen eyebeam crossed, for the roses
Had the look of flowers that are looked at.
There they were as our guests, accepted and accepting.
So we moved, and they, in a formal pattern,
Along the empty alley, into the box circle,
To look down into the drained pool.
Dry the pool, dry concrete, brown edged,
And the pool was filled with water out of sunlight,
And the lotos rose, quietly, quietly,
The surface glittered out of heart of light
And they were behind us, reflected in the pool.
Then a cloud passed, and the pool was empty.
Go, said the bird, for the leaves were full of children,
Hidden excitedly, containing laughter.
Go, go, go, said the bird: human kind
Cannot bear very much reality.
                         (11–43)

Eliot here creates a complex integration of the self with its natural surroundings that separates this passage from the doctrinally
motivated rhetorical strategies which govern the remaining sections of the poem. In conformity with Romantic modes where
landscape evokes "a varied but integral process of memory,
thought, anticipation, and feeling which remains closely inter-
volved with the outer scene,"[7] the rose garden passage isolates a
particular experience in time and space where the self enters into
correspondances with other selves or with nature. "Other echoes"
attract the poet, and a bird's voice guides his steps. The reference
to the thrush's "deception" suggests a reluctant surrender of
authorial consciousness to the forces of vision. Throughout the
passage a vocabulary of echoes, reflections, intersection, response,
and mutual acceptance corresponds to the Romantic tradition of
the interconnectedness of all things: "in response to," "the un-

seen eyebeam crossed," "our guests, accepted and accepting," "reflected in the pool."

The passage's imagery of light, childhood, music, flowers, and birds connects it to earlier poems that reveal glimpses of the poet's visionary inner world of purity. The hyacinth garden scene in *The Waste Land* offers the most obvious parallel, but there are others as well: the "vibrant air" and "unheard music" of *Burnt Norton*, for example, recall "aethereal rumours" in *The Waste Land* and "the wind's singing" in *The Hollow Men*. The children's laughter recalls a similar image in *Dans le restaurant* (*"Je la chatouillais, pour la faire rire"*) as well as *The Waste Land's* "enfants chantant dans la coupole." As usual, the way to the poet's inner Eden lies in a downward, inward direction: "Down the passage which we did not take . . . Into the rose-garden." This movement into an intimate space of enclosure, toward what Durand calls *"le centre paradisiaque"* of the psyche,[8] repeats itself later in the passage with a movement even deeper inward: "Into the boxed circle . . . down into the drained pool." The "heart of light" thus lies at the center of an enclosure within an enclosure. Narrative structure coincides with spatialization of reality as the visionary experience culminates in the arrival at this center.

Typically in Eliot's poetry, this kind of experience provokes an evaluation in terms of the poem's general ethos, which runs contrary to the processes that have led to the visionary center. Thus in *The Waste Land* the speaker's self-conscious attempt at formulating his experience—"I could not speak . . . and I knew nothing"—intrudes upon the essential purity of the vision of the "heart of light." In *Burnt Norton* a similar vision leads to a restatement of the poem's opening lines in generalized, abstract language that severs itself from the concrete and naturalistic style of the rose-garden scene: "Time past and time future / What might have been and what has been / Point to one end, which is always present." Whether or not these lines succeed in adding to the "meaning" of the visionary experience, the stylistic shift they represent clearly arises from a motivation to define the experience in purely conceptual terms. The final lines of *Burnt Norton*, part 1, constitute an extrinsic comment on the Romantic natural vision rather than a conclusion that evolves from the internal structure of the vision itself.

These lines claim for the visionary experience a status of mystical "reality" beyond the ordinary realities of human life, but Eliot's original plans for the rose-garden passage as part of *Murder in the Cathedral* locate a quite different place for this kind of experience in the poet's thought. Eliot originally wrote the first paragraph of *Burnt Norton* as a comment made by the Second Priest after the exit of Becket's Second Tempter,[9] where it would have served as a deeply nostalgic evocation of lost opportunities, "down the passage which we did not take." Becket, like the speaker in the final section of *Ash-Wednesday*, must actively resist the downward pull of such visions and put his faith in a worldly order "controlled by the order of God." In other words, the experience that in an original version of the play represents the object of temptation to be overcome, later serves in *Burnt Norton* to symbolize the object of mystical fulfillment. Such radically different uses of the same passage point to the poet's fundamental ambivalence toward his own visionary material.

The tension between Eliot's visionary language and his speculations on the nature of time point to the central conflict of his work as a whole, which strives for two radically different kinds of order: one nonlogical and intuitive, the other logical and intellectually apprehensible. In *Burnt Norton* this opposition sets the rose-garden scene against a variety of stylistic forms aimed at investing the poet's "secular epiphany"[10] with doctrinal or at least intellectual authority. Part 2, for example, opens with fifteen lines of rhymed tetrameter in a highly figurative style that establishes a classic Christian parallel between the temporal and the eternal, the earthly and the heavenly:[11] "And hear upon the sodden floor / Below, the boarhound and the boar / Pursue their pattern as before / But reconciled among the stars." The controlled symmetry of these lines, where in Dantescan manner the stars appear both at the precise center and the precise end of the strophe, corresponds to the dualistic sense of metaphysical order the passage evokes. At the same time the allegorical associations implicit in the passage contrast with the imaginative fusion of imagery in part 1. Reading these lines in conjunction with part 1, we might see them as formulating a relation between the mystical vision and the universe of cyclical change.

Such a reading would conform to traditional interpretations of the poem, as in the following statement from Helen Gardner: "The subject of the poem is an experience for which theology provides an explanation and on which religion builds a discipline, the immediate apprehension of a timeless reality, felt in time and remembered in time, the sudden revelation of 'the one end, which is always present.' "[12] Such interpretations, however, rely on the outward assertions of the poem—"Only through time time is conquered"—when the imaginative processes at work in the poem seem to counteract what the poet wishes to assert. As Graham Hough points out, nothing in the poem guarantees the theological provenance of Eliot's moments of illumination.[13] On the contrary, the stylistic differences between part 1 and part 2 of *Burnt Norton*, for example, suggest that these moments of illumination involve a radically different kind of poetic motivation from that which produces the poem's statements of doctrine.

Attempts at defining the moments of illumination in conceptual terms show not only a split between vision and doctrine, but also lead to a division of doctrinal points of view in the poem. Eliot alternately tries either to assimilate his isolated natural vision to a hierarchical "pattern" that comprehends everything between the two poles of mud and stars, or to turn it into a logical abstraction that repudiates concrete imagery and stands apart from earthly and celestial cycles:

> At the still point of the turning world,
>   Neither flesh nor fleshless;
> Neither from nor towards; at the still point,
>   there the dance is,
> But neither arrest nor movement. And do not
>   call it fixity,
> Where past and future are gathered. Neither
>   movement from nor towards,
> Neither ascent nor decline.
>   (62–66)

In its discursive and heuristic style, this passage from *Burnt Norton*, part 2, differs from both the natural vision of part 1 and the metaphorical movement from mud to stars that immediately precedes it. Here the poet's effort to understand his vision in terms of purely logical discourse leads mainly to rhetorical strategies of negation: "Neither . . . nor," "do not call it. . . ." "I cannot say where. / And I cannot say, how long, for that is to place it in time." In the repeated use of the double negative—"Neither from nor towards . . . neither arrest nor movement"—opposing terms merely cancel each other out[14] as intellectual process strives to recover intuitive experience.

This conscious abstraction of the still point or the privileged moment from ordinary notions of time and space conflicts with the doctrinal need for the visionary experience to be "involved with past and future." The mystical strain in Eliot's Christian thought adopts the ideals of absence, negation, and immobility as means of recovering vision:

> . . . not in movement
> But abstention from movement; while the world moves
> In appetency, on its metalled ways
> Of time past and time future.
>   (123–26)

Thus the "hidden laughter / Of children in the foliage." can only be "Caught in the form of limitation / Between un-being and being." Everything else in life makes up "the waste sad time / Stretching before and after."

William F. Lynch, a Jesuit theologian, shows how Eliot's insistence on the metaphysical importance of the single moment of vision, rather than on the human task of finding salvation through a life in time, involves the poet in a heretical position in relation to orthodox Christian doctrine. Lynch has also noticed the split between intellectual assent and visionary imagination in this regard:

> It seems not unseemly to suppose that Eliot's imagination (and is this not a theology?) is alive with points of *intersection* and *descent*. He seems to place our faith, our hope, and our love, not in the flux of time but in the *points* of time. I am sure his mind is interested in the line and time of Christ, whose Spirit is in his total flux. But I am not so sure about his imagination.[15]

For Lynch, as for St. Thomas, "God is act, and everything is perfect in so far as it is in act," but in the bleak time-ridden reality Eliot evokes, "any action / Is a step to the block, to the fire, down the sea's throat / Or to an illegible stone." The dissociation in Eliot's sensibility between the revelation of eternity and its consequence for human life produces, in Lynch's words, "on the one hand a further disgust for the mysteries of man and on the other the most tenuous gnostic contacts with the mysteries of God."[16] As Lynch suggests, Eliot's doctrinal tendencies correspond to a temperamental aversion to the human world, which he characterizes in a catalog of the damned that by now has become a familiar mark of Eliot's style:

> Eructation of unhealthy souls
> Into the faded air, the torpid
> Driven on the wind that sweeps the gloomy hills
>   of London,
> Hampstead and Clerkenwell, Campden and Putney,
> Highgate, Primrose and Ludgate. Not here
> Not here the darkness, in this twittering world.
>   (108–13)

Eliot's poem closely associates language with the imperfections of the human world, so that the intractability of words themselves symbolizes the unresolvable conflicts of the poet's mind. In a poem torn between the need to involve its moment of vision in universal "circulation" and a counteracting tendency to abstract the visionary experience from "this twittering world," the poet turns in frustration upon the deficiency of language:

> Not the stillness of the violin, while the note lasts,
> Not that only, but the co-existence,
> Or say that the end precedes the beginning,
> And the end and the beginning were always there
> Before the beginning and after the end.
> And all is always now. Words strain,
> Crack and sometimes break, under the burden,
> Under the tension, slip, slide, perish,
> Decay with imprecision, will not stay in place,
> Will not stay still.
>   (144–53)

In this case the attack on language follows on a series of negations, qualifications, and conjunctions between alternative ways of approaching visionary experience in purely conceptual terms.

Here, as in all of his work beginning with *Prufrock*, Eliot turns to the language of discourse in his effort to establish intellectual order. The metaphorical images of breaking, cracking, slipping, and sliding show that he seeks a language of architectural strength, rigidity, immobility, and precision. Such a conception, of course, diametrically opposes the Romantic-Symbolist tradition of ambiguity, polyvalence, and suggestion in language, including the distinctly evocative nature of the poetic symbol.

Mallarmé conceives a language whose primary principle lies in its very *"mobilité . . . étant ce qui ne se dit pas du discours."*[17] Eliot's notion of a rigid and precise language also conflicts with the image of words that "after speech, reach / Into the silence" and with the reverberating correspondences of the rose-garden passage. Here the echoes that inhabit the garden derive historically from Baudelaire's *"longs échos qui de loin se confondent"*; and when the bird calls in response to the unheard music, we see that in Eliot, too, *"Les parfums, les couleurs, et les sons se répondent."* Thus the primary division in Eliot's sensibility between intellectual and imaginative order affects not only his use of language, but also the contesting ideas of language that his poem conveys.

East Coker (published 1940) shares with *Burnt Norton* the author's ambivalence toward the material of his visionary imagination. Here, as in the earlier poem, Eliot places his natural vision alongside ideas of order expressed in terms of either allegorical structure or abstract negation. These two ordering strategies run in opposing directions, for while one joins earthly and divine purposes in the allegory of the hospital, the other works at abstracting the darkness and stillness of God from the enchainment of earthly existence—"The time of the coupling of man and woman / And that of beasts."

Eliot's natural vision, meanwhile, gets caught up in these crosscurrents and is alternately consigned to the endless flux of the turning world, or equated with the mystical stillness beyond those earthly cycles. Eliot still has trouble finding a place for the material of his visionary imagination in a universe that should conform to the ordering processes of the intellect. Once again the contending uses of language in Eliot's poem lead to a *mise en question* of language itself as the "shabby equipment" of a mind that would conquer the problem of order either by strength or submission.

The problematic vision occurs, as in *Burnt Norton*, after the introductory statement of part 1:

> In my beginning is my end. Now the light falls
> Across the open field, leaving the deep lane
> Shuttered with branches, dark in the afternoon,
> Where you lean against a bank while a van passes,
> And the deep lane insists on the direction
> Into the village, in the electric heat
> Hypnotised. In a warm haze the sultry light
> Is absorbed, not refracted, by grey stone.
> The dahlias sleep in the empty silence.
> Wait for the early owl.
>   In that open field
> If you do not come too close, if you do not come
>   too close,
> On a summer midnight, you can hear the music
> Of the weak pipe and the little drum
> And see them dancing around the bonfire
> The association of man and woman
> In daunsinge, signifying matrimonie—
> A dignified and commodiois sacrament.
> Two and two, necessarye coniunction,
> Holding eche other by the hand or the arm
> Whiche betokeneth concorde. Round and round the fire
> Leaping through the flames, or joined in circles,
> Rustically solemn or in rustic laughter. . . .
>
>   (14–35)

George Bornstein notes that this entire passage (ending with the end of part 1) conforms to the structure of greater Romantic lyrics like Wordsworth's *Tintern Abbey* and Coleridge's *The Eolian Harp*: the description of the outer landscape leads to an inner process of memory, vision, or reflection. The speaker then returns to the outer scene with renewed perception resulting from his meditative experience.[18] Bornstein also argues that the imaginative energy of the passage runs counter to Eliot's anti-Romantic tendency to see the vision either in material terms as reducing itself to "Dung and death" or in spiritual terms as symbolizing Incarnation.

Stylistic analysis supports this primarily thematic approach to the poem, for Eliot in describing his natural vision uses a different kind of language from that which evaluates the vision in conceptual or doctrinal terms. While the initial verse-paragraph of *East Coker* generalizes the human situation in an Ecclesiastes-like language of repeated conjunctions, the next section offers a concrete vision isolated in time and space: "Now the light falls / Across the open field." This language fuses subject and object in such a way that the speaker relinquishes any self-identity that would separate him from nature; intentional qualities that ordinarily form part of the perceiving mind now issue from the landscape itself. The deep lane "insists" with its own will on the direction into the village, in an "electric heat" charged with the same force as the "vibrant air" of autumn heat in *Burnt Norton*. The "Hypnotised" of line 20, ambiguous in what it modifies, further suggests the temporary surrender of the speaker's authoritative consciousness. The ambiguous subject of "Wait for the early owl" (an imperative *you*, an understood *I*, the preceding *dahlias*) emphasizes the fusion of human and natural elements. Dawn "points,"[19] like the deep lane's insistence on direction; and another day intentionally "prepares" for heat and silence. The ultimate diffusion of self-identity, the antithesis of individuation, comes at the passage's end: "I am here / Or there, or elsewhere." Jean-Paul Sartre says in an essay on Mallarmé, "*Si l'être est dispersion, l'homme en perdant son être gagne une incorruptible unité.*"[20] Eliot's imagination works differently from Mallarmé's, but we can nonetheless borrow Sartre's terms: for Eliot the dispersion of the self unites him with the purity of his natural vision.

Apart from this fusion of the human and the natural, this passage also corresponds to *Burnt Norton*, part 1, in terms of its spatial imagery. The image of "the deep lane / Shuttered with branches, dark in the afternoon" suggests the downward movement into an enclosure we have come to recognize as a topological feature of Eliot's imagination. The perimeter of the open field and the dance around the bonfire form, as in the earlier vision, a series of concentric circles with a "heart of light" at their center. The dance itself, like the antique merry-making of *Ash-*

Wednesday, part 3, creates a fragile image of sexual order—"Two and two, necessarye coniunction"—which then crumbles under the pressure of the poem's larger *ethos*:

> The time of the seasons and the constellations
> The time of milking and the time of harvest
> The time of the coupling of man and woman
> And that of beasts. Feet rising and falling.
> Eating and drinking. Dung and death.
>
> (42–46)

Eliot's repudiation of the world in time runs counter to his implicit affirmation of the privileged moment, and forces him to discredit his vision of natural order. With this repudiation the poem's language returns to the style of the introduction as it shifts from the concrete to the general, from natural description to a rhythmic repetition that winds down with shorter and shorter lexical units to three syllables of absolute reductivism: "Dung and death."

Here Eliot's authoritative consciousness denies the validity of his visionary experience, yet other parts of the poem seek to imbue the very same kind of experience with religious significance. Part 3 of *East Coker* begins with Eliot's familiar catalog of the damned—

> The captains, merchant bankers, eminent men of letters,
> The generous patrons of art, the statesmen and
>   the rulers,
> Distinguished civil servants, chairmen of many
>   committees
>
> (103–5)

—then withdraws from this world into a series of similes for the "darkness of God." Eliot follows closely the *via negativa* of Christian mystics such as St. John of the Cross and Dionysius the Pseudo-Areopagite; but his Romantic vision provides the metaphor for the soul's apprehension of God:

> So the darkness shall be the light, and the
>   stillness the dancing.
> Whisper of running streams, and winter lightning.
> The wild thyme unseen and the wild strawberry,
> The laughter in the garden, echoed ecstasy

> Not lost, but requiring, pointing to the agony
> Of death and birth.
>
> (128–33)

The scenery derives from poems like *Kubla Khan* and Shelley's *Mont Blanc*, as well as from Eliot's own earlier works (including part 1 of *Burnt Norton*).

Eliot differs from his Romantic forbears as well as his modern contemporaries, however, in the way he attaches a set of moral imperatives to his vision. The central problem of the *Four Quartets* is that these imperatives do not arise out of the material of the vision itself as they do, say, in Dante or in Augustine's *Confessions*. Eliot's poem repeatedly asserts the connection between vision and doctrine, but this matrimony lacks the *necessary* conjunction between two aspects of consciousness—a connection that other poets have established through coherent mythical or narrative frameworks.

In the face of such tensions Eliot adopts a dogmatic version of the prophetic voice of Lazarus, "come from the dead / Come back to tell you all":

> You say I am repeating
> Something I have said before. I shall say it again.
> Shall I say it again? In order to arrive there....
>
> (134–36)

The repeated formula "In order to.... You must go...." borrows the moral precepts of St. John of the Cross without recreating the kind of process by which St. John reaches them. The desire for a rationally comprehensible universe that generates this insistence on a moral meaning for his vision also underlies the heavy-handed style of part 4:

> The wounded surgeon plies the steel
> That questions the distempered part;
> Beneath the bleeding hands we feel
> The sharp compassion of the healer's art
> Resolving the enigma of the fever chart.
>
> (147–51)

This system, in which the wounded surgeon equals Christ, the dying nurse the Church, and the ruined millionaire Adam, argues the familiar notion of a divine order that resolves the apparent disorder of temporal existence. The explicitly doctrinal message of this language as well as its self-consciously allegorical style, however, completely remove it from any necessary artistic relation to the poet's natural vision. The dream of a summer midnight and the allegory of the hospital come from two radically different kinds of poetic thinking. Any integration of the two requires an extraordinary act of faith on the reader's part.

The poet's own awareness of this dramatic conflict in his consciousness creates the pathos of the *Four Quartets* and leads him ultimately to question the validity of the poetic act. For Eliot the poetic act constitutes a form of knowledge in that it seeks to define experience through language, but

> The knowledge imposes a pattern, and falsifies,
> For the pattern is new in every moment
> And every moment is a new and shocking
> Valuation of all we have been.
> (84–87)

Given this problematic relation between poetry and experience, the psychological war between intellectual order and the visionary imagination translates into an artistic war between the creative will and linguistic disorder. For Eliot the problem of a mind torn by divergent sources of inspiration becomes itself the problem of poetic composition. Thus the language and imagery of warfare provide an extended metaphor for the poet's struggle with language. In the years of *l'entre deux guerres* his own art makes a third war, a "raid on the inarticulate," with "Undisciplined squads of emotion" in a vain effort "to conquer / By strength and submission." The poet casts himself in the role of a general who, faced with mounting dissension among his troops, begins to perceive the futility of war itself.

2

In *The Dry Salvages* and *Little Gidding* (published 1941 and 1942 respectively), the continued search for a coherent poetic universe only serves to emphasize the divisions inherent in that universe and, by extension, in the poet's own identity. Like *Burnt Norton, The Dry Salvages* creates an ontological gap between the poet's Romantic natural vision and the human world, then seeks to bridge this gap by defining the vision as a "half understood" experience of Incarnation. At the same time the poem implicitly preserves its distinctions between vision and doctrine, between a Romantic use of imagery—"The wild thyme unseen, or the winter lightning / Or the waterfall"—and a more conceptual language based on notions of "prayer, observance, discipline, thought, and action." In *Little Gidding* the poet at first evaluates his natural vision as insufficient to his notion of a metaphysical absolute. Yet by juxtaposing the material of this vision to traditional Christian imagery, he finally allows it to stand as an emblem for the mystical state of being that language cannot attain. Even so, Eliot's modern sensibility lacks the cohesiveness for the apocalyptic conclusion of a *Paradiso*; the *Four Quartets* end with an expression of intense desire for the union of two kinds of experience—visionary and doctrinal, lyrical and intellectual—and the implicit renunciation of language as the vehicle of this unity.

The problematic quality of Eliot's natural vision reveals itself in the poet's simultaneous fear of and attraction to natural forces in the opening section of *The Dry Salvages*. The poem first establishes an opposition between nature and civilization that treats the river in purely conventional terms: "a conveyer of commerce," "a problem confronting the builder of bridges." As the style changes from the loosely periodic to a regular four-stress twelve-syllable line, the language becomes more subjective and imagistic:

> His rhythm was present in the nursery bedroom,
> In the rank ailanthus of the April dooryard,
> In the smell of grapes on the autumn table,
> And the evening circle in the winter gaslight.
>
> (11–14)

This Wordsworthian identification of the river with the speaker's childhood—

> That one, the fairest of all rivers, loved
> To blend his murmurs with my nurse's song
>
> (*The Prelude*, 1. 270–71)

—establishes throughout the passage an analogy not only between the human and the natural, but also between the growth of the individual and the development of a civilization that "chooses to forget" the natural forces which lie below its surface: "The river is within us." Eliot feared the potential violence of these inner forces — "sullen, untamed, and intractable" — but, like Wordsworth, he also believed in them as the embodiment of his original identity.

The movement from river to sea midway through this section enacts the typically Romantic fusion of the self with its natural surroundings: the forces within us flow out and connect us to the universe. Thus the imagery of fusion between self and nature and also among the elements of nature: the sea reaches into the granite, it tosses its contents onto the shore, and swallows men in its "dark throat." Two pure images capture the intermingling of sea, air, and earth: "The salt is on the briar rose, / The fog is in the fir trees." In its interaction with the individual, nature is endowed with intention—"The menace and caress of wave"—as well as with the power of speech—"The sea has many voices."

The use of imagery in this passage makes it poetically equivalent to the rose garden scene of *Burnt Norton* and to the vision of a summer midnight in *East Coker*. Like the earlier passages, this one points downward and inward to the origins of life, thus providing a spatial metaphor for the sources of the poet's visionary material. The poem implicitly compares the depths of the sea, with their "earlier and other creation," to the depths of the self and their association with the river and childhood. The speaker looks down into a pool to behold "The more delicate algae and the sea anemone," companions of the "ragged claws" in *Prufrock*, and the "current under sea" in *The Waste Land*. The image of the sea-pool, as well as of the nursery bedroom and the April dooryard, repeats Eliot's familiar movement into enclosed space when dealing with his visionary inner Eden. The "evening circle in the winter gaslight" conforms structurally to the dance around the bonfire in *East Coker* and the "heart of light" in the circular pool of *Burnt Norton*: all three images produce a point of light at the center of a circularly defined space.

Once having arrived at this metaphorical center of his consciousness, Eliot does not always define it the same way in terms of his rational search for order. The rose-garden scene of *Burnt*

Norton stands for a transcendent "reality" that time-ridden hu-
mankind cannot bear for long; but a similar use of imagery in
East Coker only adds fuel to Eliot's notion of an endless cycle of
human wastage. *The Dry Salvages*, like *Burnt Norton*, separates
the visionary experience from the sphere of human action in a
language that denotes a corresponding division in the poet's sensibility. On a thematic level the poem distinguishes the rhythm
of nature and the tolling sea-bell from the artificial rhythms of a
human world governed by chronometers and vain attempts to
"piece together" past and future: the distinction recalls Coleridge's discussion of organic and mechanistic forms of order. The
poem reiterates this separation on a stylistic level in shifting from
the purely imagistic language of the natural vision to a qualitatively different language of measurement, conceptual abstraction,
overt comparison, irony, and conscious paradox:

> The tolling bell
> Measures time not our time, rung by the unhurried
> Ground swell, a time
> Older than the time of chronometers, older
> Than time counted by anxious worried women
> Lying awake, calculating the future,
> Trying to unweave, unwind, unravel
> And piece together the past and the future,
> Between midnight and dawn, when the past is all
>   deception,
> The future futureless, before the morning watch
> When time stops and time is never ending.
>   (35–43)

The disjointedness of Eliot's poetic universe extends to the
problems of knowledge and meaning, which he explores in his
casually discursive passages:

> We had the experience but missed the meaning,
> And approach to the meaning restores the experience
> In a different form, beyond any meaning
> We can assign to happiness.
>   (93–96)

These various divisions between experience and meaning on one
plane, between appearance and reality on another, and finally,

between visionary imagination and intellect, conform to the notion of disconnected time in part 3, which denies the individual any single identity from one moment to the next: "You are not the same people who left that station / Or who will arrive at any terminus." Eliot typically looks outside the realm of human life for ways of ordering this fractured universe; but even this form of meaning remains potential rather than actual:

> 'on whatever sphere of being
> The mind of a man may be intent
> At the time of death'—that is the one action
> (and the time of death is every moment)
> Which shall fructify in the lives of others.
>
> (156–60)

Read in this context, the devotional verse of part 4 stands as a prayer for deliverance from a world of discontinuities, of sons or husbands "Setting forth, and not returning," of ending their voyage where the sea bell's sound "cannot reach them." In both its style and its place among the divergent energies at work in the poem, the passage corresponds to the final prayer of *Ash-Wednesday*, which seeks a way out of the conflict between the poet's attraction to nature and his devotion to God: "Suffer me not to be separated." *The Dry Salvages* seeks a similar way out of this dilemma by *equating* the poet's attraction to nature with his religious devotion. The reference in part 4 to the sea bell's "perpetual angelus," for example, assigns a doctrinal significance to the natural vision of part 1, even though the vision itself has nothing inherently Christian about it. The obvious stylistic differences between parts 1 and 4 of *The Dry Salvages* point to the independence of the poet's visionary imagination from his religiously motivated thinking, even though the poem's speaker wishes to bridge this gap between two kinds of poetic experience.

The same problem arises in part 5, where the poet separates his visionary experience of "music heard so deeply / That it is not heard at all" from the order of "prayer, observance, discipline, thought, and action," then joins the two "spheres of existence" under the idea of Incarnation. The more the poet affirms this "impossible union," however, the more these two kinds of experience seem to oppose each other in the poet's sensibility. The doctrine of Incarnation enters as a kind of deus ex machina in the drama of the poet's psyche, determined to resolve this dispute. But even at this point the "daemonic, chthonic powers" hold their ground against the forces of "right action," as the poet renews the theme of the struggle: "We are only undefeated / Because we have gone on trying."

Little Gidding comes closer than any earlier poem to uniting the powers of intellect and the visionary imagination, but it does so only by removing the poet's natural vision from "time's covenant" and juxtaposing it to the symbols of an abstract mystical reality. Mere juxtaposition, however, cannot satisfy the search for a coherent poetic identity, and the poem finally locates such an identity in a realm that lies beyond life and beyond language.

Part 1 invests the poet's vision of nature with theological significance by finding divine immanence in a particular landscape, but Eliot finally removes this experience from the true apprehension of a metaphysical Absolute:

> When the short day is brightest, with frost and fire,
> The brief sun flames the ice, on pond and ditches,
> In windless cold that is the heart's heat,
> Reflecting in a watery mirror
> A glare that is blindness in the early afternoon.
> And glow more intense than blaze of branch, or brazier,
> Stirs the dumb spirit: no wind, but pentecostal fire
> In the dark time of the year. Between melting and
>   freezing
> The soul's sap quivers. There is no earth smell
> Or smell of living thing. This is the spring time
> But not in time's covenant. Now the hedgerow
> Is blanched for an hour with transitory blossom
> Of snow, a bloom more sudden
> Than that of summer, neither budding nor fading,
> Not in the scheme of generation.
> Where is the summer, the unimaginable
> Zero summer?
>
> (4–20)

The elements of this natural vision are familiar by now. As in *Ash-Wednesday*, part 6, the poet's eye, heart, and spirit join in a kind of dialogue with nature, but *Little Gidding* adds the soul as well. The experience allows the poet to define himself momentarily in terms of the idealized nature of his visionary imagination: the soul's *sap* quivers, the heart draws its heat from the windless, sun-blazed cold. The images of reflection and response parallel the correspondences of *Burnt Norton*, part 1, in creating a fusion of subject and object. Earlier images of purity, such as the hyacinths of *The Waste Land* and Gerontion's "white feathers in the snow," come together here in the "transitory blossom of snow."

The poet separates his vision of natural purity from the time-ridden nature of dung and death, of "earth smell," and of the "scheme of generation." But he also removes it from a purely abstract ideal beyond the reach of imagination: "the unimaginable / Zero summer."[21] Once again thought conflicts with image: the unimaginable is also un-image-able,"[22] an ideal season conceived only as mathematical nullity. We may compare this bloodless tendency to intellectualize with Wallace Stevens's ability to evoke a similar ideal in chilling natural imagery:

> Perhaps, if winter once could penetrate
> Through all its purples to the final slate,
> Persisting bleakly in an icy haze.[23]

As if aware of this rupture between his natural vision and abstract conception, Eliot in the remainder of part 1 discredits conventional forms of thought and knowledge as ways of apprehending mystical reality, and begins to undermine language itself as a means of communicating this reality. The effort to recreate the visionary experience by assigning it a meaning ends in failure:

> And what you thought you came for
> Is only a shell, a husk of meaning
> From which the purpose breaks only when it is fulfilled
> If at all.
>
> (10–13)

The gap between knowledge and experience again raises the dilemma of *The Dry Salvages*:

> We had the experience but missed the meaning,
> And approach to the meaning restores the experience
> In a different form.
>
> (93–95)

These attacks on the very idea of meaning as something divorced from reality extend eventually to language itself and its inherent dependence on conventional meanings. Kenneth Burke sees the same problem from a slightly different angle: "Even if any given terminology is a *reflection* of reality, by its very nature as a terminology it must be a *selection* of reality; and to this extent it must function also as a *deflection* of reality."[24] In *Little Gidding* the speaker's response to this situation involves putting off "sense and notion" as delimiting categories that merely distract from the "communication of the dead." Such an act involves the implicit renunciation of the "language of the living" and all of the conventional assumptions on which it is based.

The poet assaults language in his attempt to reconcile the conflicting ideas of order that govern his consciousness. One form of order lies in the Romantic use of imagery that brings about a fusion of the self with its natural surroundings. Another form of order does not arise from within the process of nature, but comes from without: the dove descending on a "flame of incandescent terror," the Holy Spirit bolting from heaven "like a rush of wind"[25] and filling the disciples with strange tongues. Eliot finally conveys a Christian doctrine not of immanence of nature but of an extranatural order. *Little Gidding* portrays a poetic world in which the tension between visionary and doctrinal order can only be resolved in "a condition of complete simplicity" costing, among other things, the dismissal of language and the entire set of attachments to worldly "sense and notion" that language entails. The poem thus consigns language to the endlessly cyclical but finite "scheme of generation" that distracts from mystical experience.

Considering Eliot's awareness of language as constitutive of human reality, we can read the death of the elements in part 2 of *Little Gidding* not merely in the context of askesis—the Way of the Rejection of Images[26]—but also as a repudiation of the necessary division and categorization of reality that language provides. Notions of earth, water, air, and fire separate and divide our experience of nature, just as language separates and divides reality into finite components: "Dust in the air suspended / Marks the place where a story ended." The "familiar compound

ghost" of part 2 likewise relegates languages to the recurring cycle
of seasonal change, the confining "enchainment" of past and
future:

> Last season's fruit is eaten
> And the fullfed beast shall kick the empty pail.
>   For last year's words belong to last year's language
> And net year's words await another voice.
>   (116–20)

The speech of this "spirit unappeased and peregrine" points to
the vanity of language itself, the futility of a lifetime in which
"speech impelled us / To purify the dialect of the tribe." Rather
than provide a unified experience of the world through language,
such an enterprise has only led to further division and discord:

> First, the cold friction of expiring sense
> Without enchantment, offering no promise
>   But bitter tastelessness of shadow fruit
>   As body and soul begin to fall asunder.
> Second, the conscious impotence of rage
>   At human folly, and the laceration
>   Of laughter at what ceases to amuse.
> And last, the rending pain of re-enactment
>   Of all that you have done, and been; the shame
>   Of motives late revealed, and the awareness
> Of things ill done and done to others' harm
>   Which one you took for exercise of virtue.
>   Then fools' approval stings and honor stains.
>   (131–43)

A momentary digression from the subject of *Little Gidding's*
attacks on language can offer a possible explanation for both the
rigid structure and the intensely bitter language of this speech. In
the manuscript drafts to part 2 of *Little Gidding,* one finds the
only instance of a sustained passage originally written for the
Four Quartets but dropped in the final version. The thirty lines
of the speech (lines 120–49) revealing the painful "gifts reserved
for age" do not appear in the first draft of *Little Gidding.* In their
place the wandering spirit offers a very different sort of counsel,
which demonstrates a highly ambiguous feeling toward experiences of richly sensual awareness:

Remember rather the essential moments
  That were the times of birth and death and change
  The agony and the solitary vigil.
Remember also fear, loathing and hate,
  The wild strawberries eaten in the garden,
  The walls of Poitiers, and the Anjou wine,
The fresh new season's rope, the smell of varnish
  On the clear oar, the drying of the sails,
Such things as seem of least and most importance.
So, as you circumscribe this dreary round,
  Shall your life pass from you, with all you hated
  And all you loved, the future and the past.[27]

These images of light and air and color faintly recall some of
the most brilliantly lyrical passages of earlier poems, but here
their force is weakened by both syntactical and semantic elements. The catalog form trivializes the nature of the experience
evoked by these images, while the passage as a whole neutralizes
them by associating them simultaneously with life's "essential
moments" and memories of "fear, loathing, and hate." Once
again, it is as if Eliot, fearing the power and freedom of his own
imagination, had sought to defuse in his poetry the force of that
which moved him most profoundly. One cannot help wondering
whether Eliot's decision to suppress this passage was made not
only because of its technical mediocrity, but also because it ex-
poses in especially crude form a conflict inherent in all of his
work.

From this perspective, the final version of the speech, with its
relentless enumeration of losses and its emphasis on extinguished
sense and emotion, stands as a brutal renunciation of those moments of "enchantment," as well as a comment on the futility of
language itself.

One of the ironies of Eliot's poetry lies in the way its stylistic
structure often undermines its thematic content. For example,
part 2 of *Little Gidding* proclaims the death of the four elements in such a way as to reinforce an elemental view of the
world. Air, earth, water, and fire are treated in orderly succession,
creating a series of textual divisions that reasserts the divisional
view of nature. The last line of each stanza ends with the name
of its element, so that the element, at least in a textual sense,

survives its own sentence (using both meanings of *sentence*). The Dantescan "familiar compound ghost" finally points to the realm of fulfilled being "Where you must move in measure, like a dancer"; yet the ghost himself is still serving time in the Inferno of endless succession: his speech itself proceeds "From wrong to wrong" as it discloses "the gifts reserved for age" in numerative order. The enumerative style divides and apportions life in such a way as to prevent the vision of unified being suggested by the image of the dancer and by the interaction with nature in part 1. Part 3 compounds the divided view of reality, as it enumerates the "three conditions which often look alike" and elaborates on this division with the use of precept and example: "This is the use of memory. . . . Thus. . . ."

Eliot's mind works this way, yet at the same time he sees the weakness of a language made up of "sense and notion," "thought and theory"; this will never recapture the "glow more intense than blaze of branch, or brazier" that haunts the poet's imagination. The only resolution of this factional rivalry of the mind lies not in speech but in silence:

> We cannot revive old factions
> We cannot restore old policies
> Or follow an antique drum.
> These men, and those who opposed them
> And those whom they opposed
> Accept the constitution of silence
> And are folded in a single party.
> (185–91)

Beginning with the slippage and decay of words in *Burnt Norton* and continuing through the "intolerable wrestle / With words and meanings" of *East Coker*, the *Four Quartets* continually lay siege to the idea of language itself. The fifth movement of *Little Gidding* pronounces the final obituary on language by consigning it to the larger flux of life in time. Language itself establishes its own internal order, "where every word is at home / Taking its place to support the others," but like the consort of dancers around the bonfire, it returns to the scheme of successive death and generation: "Every poem an epitaph." The poem opposes the sum of all language and action against images of mystical communication: the hieroglyphic "illegible stone," the "voice of the hidden waterfall" only half heard in a moment of silence: "in the stillness / Between two waves of the sea." But even the communication of the dead implies, in its very function as language, a duality of signifier and signified, speaker and hearer. The poet will have achieved oneness with his mystical being when this language, too, no longer needs speaking: "When the tongues of flame are in-folded."

Traditional readings tend to see the end of this poem as a triumphant resolution, at least in some future "end of all our exploring," of the poet's spiritual quest: a reconciliation of the temporal and the eternal, of human suffering and divine love. As we have seen before, however, the surface statements in Eliot's poems frequently claim such resolutions without having developed a textual unity that would make them wholly convincing. Wherever the poem asserts that the boarhound and the boar are "reconciled among the stars," that old factions are "folded into a single party," or that "the fire and the rose are one," we must ask whether the text actually brings about this unification or whether, on the other hand, the poet simply invokes this ideal as an impassioned response to the actual experience of textual, psychological, and metaphysical disunity.

The kind of analysis we have undertaken here must consider the underlying motivations of these overt affirmations in terms of Eliot's efforts to create his own coherent poetic identity. Does the lyrical eloquence of the poem's final strophe resolve the psychological conflicts riddling each of the *Quartets*? Does the poet finally achieve, even potentially, the unity of being he has sought ever since the psychic divisions of *Prufrock*? Given the grounds on which he beseeches such unity, it can at best represent here only a consummation devoutly to be wished. Hence the essentially *optative* mood of these lines: the Tennysonian courage of the voice proclaiming, "We shall not cease from exploration," the studied calmness of tone overall, the repeated assurances from an earlier Christian mystic that "all shall be well and / All manner of thing shall be well." Despite these affirmations, the poet still seeks a way to reconcile the private inner Eden embodied in his natural vision—"the children in the apple tree"— with the doctrinal structure his mind has embraced. Like the final prayer of *Ash-Wednesday*, this prayer, too, is uttered against the background of psychic disunity.

The frequency and intensity of Eliot's Romantic use of imagery in separate passages throughout the *Four Quartets* provide a series of structurally and psychologically central passages in which the poet surrenders self-consciousness in a dreamlike natural vision. Earlier poems, as if afraid of pursuing the vision, treated it with Prufrockian irony, buried it among the fragments of *The Waste Land* or, as in *Ash-Wednesday*, identified it with sin and heresy: "Suffer us not to mock ourselves with falsehood." The *Four Quartets* renew the struggle with an unruly imagination by comparing its vision to dangerous natural forces, by condemning it to the cycle of "dung and death" or, finally, by interpreting it as a sign of divine Incarnation.

This last strategy nearly succeeds in bringing together Eliot's rage for intellectual order with the independent, almost demonic order of his vision. Given the polar opposition of these values in Eliot's sensibility, however, the best he can do is to place them side by side in his poetic language, and pray for their union in some ideal realm. The final movement of *Little Gidding*, for example, juxtaposes a language motivated by religious concept, "With the drawing of this Love and the voice of this Calling," with images derived from moments of natural vision:

> At the source of the longest river
> The voice of the hidden waterfall
> And the children in the apple-tree
> Not known, because not looked for
> But heard, half-heard, in the stillness
> Between two waves of the sea.
> (246–51)

The surface logic of the poem equates the two passages as pointing to a similar phenomenon in Eliot's poetic universe, but the very difference in the way language is used reveals the deeper division in Eliot's consciousness.

Eliot's is an orthodox Christian mind cursed with an intensely Romantic imagination. In this context the final lines of the *Four Quartets* read as a Symbolist cry for psychic unity—"*Rends-moi ... la treille où le pampre à la rose s'allie*"[28]—combined with an instinctive mysticism that knows *"la vraie vie est absente."* "The poetry does not matter." Eliot, like Mallarmé, knows that even the language of poetry, corrupted with meanings inherited from a world of disorder, cannot ultimately attain to the immaculate purity of his absent mystical reality. His last great poem proclaims the death of language, and stands as a commitment to his search for unity of the self in "the constitution of silence."

NOTES

1. Spender, *T. S. Eliot*, p. 132.
2. Thomas R. Rees, *The Technique of T. S. Eliot* (The Hague: Mouton, 1974), p. 304.
3. Benamou, *Wallace Stevens and the Symbolist Imagination*, p. 111.
4. Helen Gardner, *The Composition of "Four Quartets"* (New York: Oxford University Press, 1978), p. 118. See also a similarly devised scheme for *Little Gidding*, ibid., p. 157.
5. Cf. Wimsatt, "Romantic Nature Imagery," pp. 77–88.
6. Cf. Bornstein, *Transformations of Romanticism*, p. 106; Frank Kermode, *Romantic Image* (London: Routledge & Kegan Paul, 1957), pp. 138–61; Stead, *The New Poetic*, pp. 96–122.
7. M. H. Abrams, "Structure and Style in the Greater Romantic Lyric," in Bloom, *Romanticism and Consciousness*, p. 201. See also n. 5 above.
8. Durand, *Les Structures anthropologiques de l'imaginaire*, p. 261.
9. Gardner, *The Composition of "Four Quartets,"* p. 39.
10. The term is used by Graham Hough in "Vision and Doctrine in *Four Quartets*," *Critical Quarterly* 15 (Summer 1973):107–28.
11. One finds such a parallel in St. Thomas Aquinas, *Book of the Blessed Dionysius Concerning the Divine Names*, vii, lect. 4: "By means of the ordering of all things, which has been as it were projected out of Him and which bears certain images and likenesses of its divine patterning, we ascend in ordered degrees so far as we are able to that which is above all things . . . and the conception of a universal cause." Cited in Raymond Preston, *"Four Quartets" Rehearsed* (London: Sheed & Ward, 1948), p. 16.
12. C. K. Stead, *"Four Quartets: A Commentary,"* in Rajan, *T. S. Eliot: A Study of His Writings*, p. 63.
13. Hough, "Vision and Doctrine in *Four Quartets*," p. 114.
14. This observation is made by Finn Bille, in "The Ultimate Metaphor and the Defeat of Poetry in T. S. Eliot's *Four Quartets*," *International Journal of Symbology* 3 (March 1972):17.

15. Lynch, *Christ and Apollo*, p. 172. The emphasis is in the original.

16. Ibid., 176.

17. Stéphane Mallarmé, *Oeuvres complètes* (Paris: Pléiade, 1945), p. 386.

18. Bornstein, *Transformations of Romanticism*, p. 156. See also Abrams, "Greater Romantic Lyric," p. 201.

19. Eliot draws on the French verb *poindre*, as in *le matin point* (the dawn breaks) in creating a new use of the English verb *to point*.

20. Sartre's preface to Stéphane Mallarmé, *Poésies* (Paris: Gallimard, 1972), p. 10.

21. The "Zero summer" is etymologically as well as thematically related to the "still point" of the *Four Quartets* in suggesting either an apex or a mathematical center. On the summer solstice (June 21) the sun is farthest from the equator or highest in the sky for those living in the northern hemisphere. The *Oxford English Dictionary* also provides as one meaning of the verb *to summer*: "To radiate from or converge towards a centre, like the joints of an arch."

22. Bille, "The Ultimate Metaphor," p. 22.

23. Wallace Stevens, *Collected Poems* (New York: Alfred Knopf, 1957), p. 96.

24. Kenneth Burke, *Language as Symbolic Action* (Berkeley: University of California Press, 1966), p. 45. The emphasis is in the original.

25. Acts 2:2, the basis for the Christian celebration of Pentecost.

26. Spanos, " 'Wanna Go Home, Baby?' " p. 14.

27. Gardner, *The Composition of "Four Quartets,"* p. 183. The passage continues:

> United to another past, another future,
>   (After many seas and after many lands)
>   The dead and the unborn, who shall be nearer
> Than the voices and the faces that were most near.
>   This is the final gift of earth accorded—
>   One soil, one past, one future, in one place.
> Nor shall the eternal thereby be remoter
>   But nearer: seek or seek not, it is here.
>   Now, the last love on earth. The rest is grace.
> He turned away, and in the autumn weather
>   I heard a distant dull deferred report
>   At which I started: and the sun had risen.

28. Gerard de Nerval, *El Desdichado*, in *Les Chimères* (Paris: Garnier-Flammarion, 1965), p. 239.

CHAPTER FIVE

To Analyze the Critic

As a critic Eliot constantly evaluated the creative work of
other writers by the degree to which they had confronted or
solved the particular problem he himself faced as a poet: the
struggle to salvage an artistic whole from the battleground of his
own consciousness. In a dialetical notion of the artistic process
that relates (however unintentionally) to Blake's figures of the
Prolific and the Devourer or to Coleridge's Free Life and confining Form,[1] Eliot conceives of a ruling critical faculty in endless dispute with an involuntary creative impulse in the labor of
the artist. In Eliot's own mythology of mind this critical faculty
represents a force for intellectual order in the way it disciplines
an essentially formless and potentially dangerous poetic material.
Thus Dante, always Eliot's artistic and spiritual model, achieves
an *"ordered scale* of human emotions"[2] (*SW*, 168; the emphasis
is mine), while Blake's poetry suffers from not being "controlled
by a respect for impersonal reason . . . for the objectivity of science" (*SE*, 279).

But quite apart from this overt critical approach and more important for our study of Eliot's artistic consciousness, the style
and imagery of his critical essays reveal the same inner conflict
that surfaced in the poems: a rivalry between intellectual order
and a purely visionary imagination for the poet's allegiance. This
conflict of values thus emerges in Eliot's writing not only as an

This chapter originally appeared as "T. S. Eliot's Divided Critical Sensibility"
in *Criticism* 23 (Winter 1981) and is reprinted here with slight changes by permission of the publisher.

object of critical inquiry and evaluation in the work of other writers, but also as a characteristic of Eliot's own criticism. Throughout Eliot's career one finds a continual slippage in the style of his essays toward covert identification with the very artistic values that a more conscious critical position opposes.

The following pages trace the evolution of this conflict while dividing Eliot's history as literary and social critic into three stages: the early years leading up to and immediately following publication of *The Waste Land,* the middle years surrounding Eliot's religious conversion, when he edited the *Criterion,* and the final years (beginning with the late 1930s) as elder statesman to the world of letters. My examination of the changing nature of Eliot's critical sensibility at each successive stage begins with a synoptic account of the crucial forces then at work in his criticism and culminates in a more detailed analysis of two essays from that same period—one on a general topic (e.g., *After Strange Gods*) and one on a specific writer ("Lancelot Andrewes"). The six essays chosen for closer consideration all form part of the Eliotic canon in the sense that scholars have traditionally considered them as part of the mainstream of his critical thought; the range of subjects they address suggests that the conflict they reveal in Eliot's basic critical approach was not limited to his treatment of a particular author or period in history.

We should distinguish the methodology inherent in this reading of Eliot's criticism from conventional readings concerned primarily with an exposition of "the standards he proposed and the principles on which they rested."[3] Instead, my reading focuses less on *what* Eliot said than on *the way* he said it, on the theory that structural elements in prose, such as shifts in style and patterns of imagery, serve as an index to the structure of the consciousness informing them. Once again George Bornstein provides a precedent for this kind of reading in his analysis of the psychological motivations underlying Eliot's changing critical evaluations of the English Romantic poets.[4]

1

Eliot's early criticism entrenches notions of empirical objectivity and the power of human intellect as defenses against the danger of primitive emotion or feeling. His youthful attraction to philosophical Realism[5] and the Imagists' emphasis on the use of concrete visual images led Eliot to value, at least outwardly, an art based on "facts" and "experience." A 1919 review of Yeats's *The Cutting of an Agate*[6] objects that "we do not see either his thought or his feeling grow out of human experience." Irish literature in general suffers from not having had to face "direct contacts"; Yeats himself has "feeling," but "the objects upon which it is directed are not fixed." The conscious operations of the human mind should insure against being swallowed up by Yeats's fantastic dream world. Thus Ben Jonson's "conscious and deliberate" mind creates a world where "the ruling faculty is a critical perception, a commentary upon experienced feeling and sensations" (*SE*, 132).

The language of intellect naturally engages the metaphors of science. A 1920 essay on Dante (*SW*, 159) speaks of poetry penetrated by a philosophical idea as "almost a physical modification" of that idea. The same essay locates a "centre of gravity" of human emotion and notes the usefulness of Dante's allegory and astronomy as a "mechanical framework" for his poem. The famous essay on "The Metaphysical Poets" claims that to look into our hearts and write is not looking deep enough: "One must look into the cerebral cortex, the nervous system, and the digestive tracts" (*SE*, 250).

In a critical style strewn with images of violence, Eliot arrays this language of scientific precision against the dark forces rising from the depths of the psyche. The essay on Jonson connects the arousal of "swarms of inarticulate feelings" with "the lazy reader's fatuity" (*SE*, 128); but it notes that unlike Jonson's, the works of Shakespeare, Donne, and Webster "have often a network of tentacular roots reaching down to the deepest terrors and desires" (*SE*, 135). Blake as a poet is "naked" and thus "terrifying," but "formlessness attacks his draughtsmanship," and the ideas of his later poetry suffer from a lack of "prolonged manipulation." The famous dissociation of sensibility that set in after the age of metaphysical poetry brought a refinement of language in later poetry, but "the feeling became more crude" (*SE*, 247). Poets of the Romantic period revolted against the "ratiocinative," and "they thought and felt by fits, unbalanced."

Eliot repeatedly defends the use of force, of "material compelled into unity by the operation of the poet's mind" as a metaphor for the poetic act: the poet must be willing "to force, to dislocate if necessary, language into his meaning" (*SE*, 248). The primary theme running through this line of Eliot's thought is one of control over a range of primitive human impulses variously labelled as nebulous feelings, narcotic fancies, and hallucination. The poet's task, as described in a 1923 essay on "The Function of Criticism," lies in reducing all of these impulses to "something precise, tractable, *under control*" (*SE*, 20; the emphasis is mine).

The central conflict in Eliot's thinking lies not, however, in this classic opposition between Prolific and Devourer, but in his ambivalence toward the progeny cf the Prolific. He finds both an octopus and an angel dwelling in the darker regions of the mind: an object of horror as well as the source of the purest poetic vision. Thus the repressive tendencies of Eliot's critical thought compete with an equally powerful fascination with unconscious material as the original source of creative inspiration. As early as 1917 Eliot praises the "evident sincerity" of Rimbaud's *Illuminations* "as if rising immediately and unreflectingly from the core of man's feeling."[7] In Jonson he finds a power that "comes from below the intellect," but he recognizes that Shakespeare's characters represent "a more complex tissue of feelings and desires" and "emotion deeper and more obscure" (*SE*, 137). He partly redeems Blake for "a gift of hallucinated vision" (*SE*, 279), and even Swinburne proves capable of "a tremendous statement, like statements made in our dreams" (*SE*, 284).

One finds evidence of an inner dissension regarding the nature of the creative imagination in practically everything Eliot wrote. Even so imposing an article of Eliotic faith as "Tradition and the Individual Talent" (1919) reveals a crucial uneasiness concerning the role of the unconscious in the poetic act. The essay starts by establishing primacy of the ordering intellect in the artistic process, but it later undermines this position by locating the source of artistic creation in darker regions of the mind. Eliot's scientific dissection of the artistic process ends by relying paradoxically on an almost mystical notion of imaginative vision. The kind of reading I have undertaken seeks to define the underlying assumptions of statements like "Poetry is not a turning loose of emotion, but an escape from emotion" (*SW*, 58). The expression *turning loose* denotes a potential for violence, while the statement as a whole suggests a characteristic fear of irrational forces in the artistic process.

The first half of Eliot's essay reads as an elaborate defense against these forces that surface here as either "emotion" or "personality." Eliot describes tradition above all as an *active* force for order, operating not only historically but also in the mind and work of the artist. Dead poets "assert their immortality most vigorously," the historical sense "compels" a man to write a certain way, the poet will be "judged, not amputated" by standards of the past. This language carries an undercurrent of violence, an active struggle within the mind of the individual artist. Aware of the standards by which he will be judged, the artist must "sweat" for his knowledge if necessary, must "surrender" himself: "The progress of an artist is a continual self-sacrifice, a continual extinction of personality." Prolific and Devourer are transformed here into self and tradition.

The terms of this opposition recall other instances in which Eliot sets the order of a conscious intellect against less controllable elements of the creative process; here, indeed, he repeatedly associates tradition with objective mental awareness rather than with instinct or the material of dreams. A writer must be "acutely conscious" of his place in time and "very conscious of the main current" of the past. Eliot embodies tradition in intellectual terms as "the mind of Europe" and insists on the writer's continual awareness of this external source of order—"much more important than his own private mind"—as a model for individual artistic development.

In ways that point to the divisive tension of his critical sensibility, Eliot in part 2 of "Tradition and the Individual Talent" reverses the direction of his initial argument by relegating the mind to a passive role in the creative act and by describing this process as a surrender to the workings of the unconscious. At the same time he neutralizes the potential danger of the unconscious by separating it into independent components and discussing these in scientific terms.

In a kind of laboratory analysis of the poetic act, Eliot compares the mind of the poet to a shred of platinum that remains "inert, neutral, and unchanged" during the combination of oxygen and sulphur dioxide into sulphurous acid. The solid mind must be present during the artistic process either as catalyst or as "receptacle," but the real action takes place between gaseous "emotions and feelings." What Eliot means by emotion is difficult to pin down,[8] but feelings clearly act independently of conscious motivation. Eliot sees these mysterious feelings as "floating," "in suspension" in the poet's mind; they come into play only at fortuitous moments, depending not on the poet's choice but on "the right combination" of artistic elements. This unconscious substance holds the essence of poetic material, such that "great poetry may be made . . . composed out of feelings solely" (*SW*, 54). Eliot further says of poetry that "it is a concentration which does not happen consciously or of deliberation. These experiences are not 'recollected', and they finally unite in an atmosphere which is 'tranquil' only in that it is a passive attending upon the event" (*SW*, 58).

Eliot of course states the opposite view many times. In "The Function of Criticism" he ridicules "the thesis that the great artist is the unconscious artist, unconsciously inscribing on his banner the words Muddle Through" (*SE*, 18). But we do not have to discover the logical inconsistencies of Eliot's work to see the conflicting priorities in his critical thought: how the poet's conscious need for external order in the form of tradition counters his necessary surrender to the internal order of his own unconscious. We have seen another side of this dispute in the way Eliot's radically empirical dissection of the artistic process, with its dismissal of any "semiethical criterion of 'sublimity,' " finally locates the source of poetry in the miraculous and unknown regions of the irrational.

Eliot's essay on "Hamlet and His Problems" (1919) shows even more clearly this discrepancy between ways of talking about art, where the foundations of a purely rational criticism gradually collapse into the recesses of a more deeply excavated psychic terrain. On one level the lapsed philosophy student borrows the language of logical positivism to support essentially classical values of stable proportion, unity of dramatic action, and artistic decorum in adjusting language to its object: "The only way of expressing emotion in the form of art is by finding an 'objective

correlative'; in other words, a set of objectives, a situation, a chain
of events which shall be the formula of that *particular* emotion;
such that when the external facts, which must terminate in sensory experience, are given, the emotion is immediately evoked"
(*SW*, 100). The insistence on "external facts," "sensory experience" and the formulaic function of art reflects a positivist bias
that later in the same paragraph speaks of Shakespeare's play in
terms of "the *données* of the problem" and "objective equiva-
lence." Yet, despite the scientific precision that Eliot's style implies, the principle that he invokes really goes little beyond classical norms which prescribe the appropriateness of expression to
underlying sentiment: "*Souvent trop d'abondance apprauvit la
matière.*"[9]

Eliot's elaborate display of objectivity in discussing the artistic
process may momentarily divert our attention from the strong
undercurrent of fear and violence that runs through the essay
"Hamlet and His Problems." What eventually develops as a
metaphor for the critic's instability starts out rather innocently
as a discussion of Shakespeare's historical sources: "we perceive
his *Hamlet* to be superposed upon much cruder material which
persists even in the final form" (*SW*, 97). In the next paragraph
this "intractable" material still refers to the work of Shakespeare's
forbears, but Eliot quickly turns this anxiety of influence into an
inner wrestling match between the artist and his own psyche:
"*Hamlet*, like the sonnets, is full of some stuff that the writer
could not drag to light, contemplate, or manipulate into art"
(*SW*, 100). Now this intractable material, no longer simply a
problem of adapting earlier versions of the Hamlet myth, takes
on a demonic role in the drama of the poet's imagination. The
rational, positivist language Eliot has adopted for his definition of
the objective correlative gives way to violent imagery. He treats
Hamlet's dominating emotion in terms of some all-consuming
mythical monster: it "envelops and exceeds" his mother, it remains "to poison life and obstruct action," no action can satisfy
it. Under some unknown compulsion Shakespeare attempted to
express "the inexpressibly horrible."

Eliot's claim that the motivating force of the play exceeds the
play's actions and words reveals a critical position that includes
its own contradiction. In the language of semiotics, Eliot com-

plains of the inadequacy of the signifier to the signified. Yet his vivid awareness of the nature of the signified demonstrates that it has received adequate signification. Eliot really wants a better defense against the forces of madness that surface only too clearly in Shakespeare's play and that Shakespeare has allowed to shape the main character and his actions. Eliot offers his notion of the objective correlative as a possible means of controlling these dark powers, just as his critical emphasis on external facts functions, however ineffectively, as a defense against his personal involvement in the struggle he ascribes to Hamlet. In the end, though, Eliot abandons any pretense of limiting this condition to the case of Hamlet or even to Shakespeare: "The intense feeling, ecstatic or terrible, without an object or exceeding its object, is something which every person of sensibility has known: it is doubtless a study to pathologists" (SW, 100). Once again Eliot shows his ambivalence toward the power of the unconscious. By this point the "crude material" has evolved from a problem of artistic composition into an overpowering force of destruction, and finally to a universal source of artistic creation. Eliot says of this ecstatic or terrible feeling that the artist "keeps it alive by his ability to intensify the world to his emotions." As everywhere in Eliot's work, the visionary power of the unconscious rises up to challenge the rational order of the intellect.

A passage in *The Use of Poetry and the Use of Criticism* (1932) likens the age of Dryden and the age of Wordsworth to the alternating sides of a schizophrenic mind: "What I see, in the history of English poetry, is not so much daemonic possession as the splitting up of personality" (*UPUC*, 84). The observation may be commonplace, but the choice of words indicates Eliot's historical awareness of a condition that effectively defines his own thought and work.

The nature of this division in Eliot's consciousness of course changes through time. The early essays both described and enacted the battle between a conscious intellect and the horrifying but visionary forces of the unconscious. There the force for intellectual order consisted primarily of the mind itself and its "objective" relationship to external reality. In the years surrounding his religious conversion in 1927, Eliot's critical tactic depends less on the defensive capabilities of the intellect alone than on the kind of order residing in philosophical, cultural, and religious institutions; the mind's defense against its own primitive impulses now entails their subordination to a "coherent system" of thought and belief.

For example, Eliot pointed out in his essay "Dante" (1929) that the *Divine Comedy* has a Christian scheme behind it which, through the allegorical method, provides for a controlled organization of human passions: "Every degree of the feeling of humanity, from lowest to highest, has . . . an intimate relation to the next above and below, and all fit together according to the logic of sensibility" (*SE*, 229). In his essay on the poetry of Baudelaire ("Baudelaire," 1930), on the other hand, Eliot found "the content of feeling . . . constantly bursting the receptacle" (*SE*, 375) partly because of the poet's imperfect conception of Good and Evil and partly because his notion of beatitude tended to the "wishy-washy" (*SE*, 380). The 1931 essay on "The *Pensées* of Pascal" offers a precise formulation of the way Eliot's critical sensibility developed from a reliance on conscious objectivity to an acceptance of Christian dogma. It reveals Eliot's Christianity as being primarily a structure for intellectual order: "The Christian thinker . . . proceeds by rejection and elimination. He finds the world to be so and so; he finds its character inexplicable by any non-religious theory: among religions he finds Christianity, and Catholic Christianity, to account most satisfactorily for the world and especially for the moral world within" (*SE* 360). Such a system of belief does not entirely exclude emotion, for Pascal can be passionate, "but passionate only through a powerful and regulated intellect" (*SE*, 363). This defensive function of ideological structure resurfaces in "Religion and Literature" (1935), in which Eliot associates theological and moral principles in the reader of poetry with a "critical power which protects us from excessive possession by any one literary personality" (*SE*, 349).

As the use of words like *passion* and *possession* suggests, the language of psychic conflict in these middle years of Eliot's career gains in sexuality what it loses in overt violence. Although the struggle is no less intense, Eliot now sees the artistic sensibility as battling not the Medusa but the Sirens of its own unconscious. Eliot repeatedly compares aesthetic to sexual experience. Even the reading of a poem is "like our intenser experiences of other human beings"; it includes an early moment of "shock and surprise, even of terror" (*SE*, 212). Eliot recalls his own early "craving" for poetry at the age of puberty and how with a reading of Fitzgerald's *Omar* "the world appeared anew, painted with bright, delicious and painful colours" (*UPUC*, 33). The use of sexual imagery allows Eliot to trivialize one aspect of his own sensibility by assigning it to the adolescent mind, but it also suggests a latent attraction to the forces of the irrational, and even a dependence on them as the true source of artistic inspiration. Thus he speaks of Dante's "brave attempts to fabricate something permanent and holy out of his personal animal feelings" and Shakespeare's "struggle—which alone constitutes life for the poet—to transmute his personal and private agonies into something rich and strange" (*SE*, 117).

After Strange Gods (1933)[10] redefines the questions dealt with in "Tradition and the Individual Talent" in the light of Eliot's religious and intellectual development over a fifteen-year period. At the same time it redraws the battle lines of the critic's war against himslf. In part 1 of this three-part essay, Eliot appears to have broadened his concept of tradition to include not only literary monuments but "all those habitual actions, habits and customs" worth preserving from a civilized past. But, in fact, this new concept represents a narrowing of Eliot's earlier views, in its exclusionary nature. Eliot dreams of a homogeneous native culture free of "the influx of foreign populations" and unadulterated by religious differences. We read with embarrassment that "reasons of race and religion combine to make any number of free-thinking Jews undesirable" (*ASG*, 20). Under the subtitle "A Primer of Modern Heresy," Eliot's essay verges on the pathological in the way it focuses on Jews, Liberals, workers, and degenerate writers like D. H. Lawrence as causes or symptoms of disorder in modern life. Bornstein's argument that Eliot's anti-Semitism results from anxiety over his own inner identity[11] can be extended to account for Eliot's fear of all those cultural elements which threaten his modernized version of the pastoral society. As if confessing his own vulnerability to such elements, Eliot warns that "heresy is apt to have a seductive simplicity, to make a direct and persuasive appeal to intellect and emotions, and to be altogether more plausible than the truth" (*ASG*, 26).

In his 1919 essay Eliot simply urged the individual artist's conscious awareness of tradition, but by 1933 he had strengthened
the protective power of this awareness by raising it to the level of
orthodoxy—Eliot's word for the conscious cultivation of tradition
within a Christian moral framework. The forces of intellectual
order thus have an entire arsenal of Christian doctrine to fall
back upon.

Parts 2 and 3 of *After Strange Gods* launch an attack on the
heresies of Eliot's contemporaries, where the greatest danger lies
in the post-Romantic notion that poetry can replace religion in
modern life. Eliot argues against this substitution on the quite
logical grounds that it will destroy our capacity for ethical judgment by making one man's view of life as good as another's
(ASG, 34). But his actual treatment of this heresy in the works
of other writers indicates another motivation: Eliot cannot accept
the replacement of religion by poetry, because the poetic process
breaks the seal of consciousness and sets free the unknown forces
within; it takes us beyond limits better observed for the sake of
emotional stability. Religion—at least of the sort that Eliot admires—provides a structure for intellectual control.

This fear of relinquishing a controlling authorial consciousness
pervades Eliot's discussion of the work of individual artists. Eliot
quotes from an early poem of Yeats, in which he finds a "deliberate evocation of trance"; he then produces, as Yeats's "confession," a passage in "The Symbolism of Poetry" stating that the
purpose of rhythm is "to keep us in that state of perhaps real
trance, in which the mind liberated from the pressure of the will
is unfolded in symbols" (ASG, 49). I. A. Richards takes the
stand to testify that Yeats "is uncertain because he has adopted
as a technique of inspiration the use of trance, of dissociated
phases of consciousness, and the revelations given in these dissociated states are insufficiently connected with normal experience"
(ASG, 50). That judgment would have sufficed for Eliot in 1919,
but the orthodox Christian carries Richards's complaint further
by adding: "Mr. Yeats's 'supernatural world' was the wrong supernatural world. It was not a world of spiritual significance, not
a world of real Good and Evil, but a highly sophisticated lower
mythology summoned, like a physician, to supply the fading

pulse of poetry with some transient stimulant so that the dying patient may utter his last words" (ASG, 50). One suspects this trial would not have been necessary had the offender's sorcery not affected the judge so powerfully.

Even the seemingly harmless Thomas Hardy, with his "period peasants pleasing to the metropolitan imagination," does not escape Eliot's Jesuitical wrath. The "extreme emotionalism" of Hardy's characters seems to Eliot "a symptom of decadence": "The work of the late Thomas Hardy represents an interesting example of a powerful personality *uncurbed* by any institutional attachment or by *submission* to any objective beliefs" (ASG, 59; the emphasis is mine). This language points once again to the defensive strategy involved in Eliot's adherence to an institutional guarantee of intellectual order. The strategy comes into play as a direct result of Eliot's intense responsiveness to Hardy's cultivation of horror and emotion, a kind of involuntary sympathy that makes Hardy's work "a refined form of self-torture on the part of the reader" (ASG, 61).

Yeats and Hardy provide Eliot with occasions for light skirmishing; but Eliot saves his heavy ammunition for D. H. Lawrence. Lawrence drove Eliot to distraction. The author of *Women in Love* and *Fantasia of the Unconscious* shows "an incapacity for what we ordinarily call thinking," a "distinct sexual morbidity," and an "insensibility to ordinary social morality" so alien to Eliot's mind that he is baffled by it as "a monstrosity" (ASG, 64). Eliot writes of his contemporary that "an untrained mind, and a soul destitute of humility and filled with self-righteousness, is a blind servant and a fatal leader" (ASG, 64). *Lady Chatterley's Lover* excites Eliot's disgust on both sexual and social counts: "Our old acquaintance, the game-keeper, turns up again: the social obsession which makes his well-born—or almost well-born—ladies offer themselves to—or make use of—plebians springs from the same morbidity which makes other of his female characters bestow their favors upon savages. The author of that book seems to me to have been a very sick man indeed" (ASG, 66).

Eliot reacts all the more violently for his obvious attraction to Lawrence, who emerges from these pages as a modern version of the Miltonic Satan. Eliot regards Lawrence as "a very much greater genius" than Hardy; he notes his "keen sensibility and capacity for profound intuition," although he hastens to add that Lawrence drew the wrong conclusions from this intuition. Having started life "wholly free from any restriction of tradition or institution," he states, Lawrence displayed a "lust" for intellectual independence that eventually made him an agent of Hell: "The daemonic powers found an instrument of far greater range, delicacy, and power in the author of *The Prussian Officer* [Lawrence] than in the author of *A Group of Noble Dames* [Hardy]" (*ASG*, 65). Of course, these very demonic powers—Lawrence's dark forces of blood-consciousness—have been from the beginning the object of Eliot's fear and obsession. As their servant, Lawrence holds an attraction that Eliot needs the support of doctrine to resist: "Where there is no external test of a writer's work . . . we may be simply yielding ourselves to one seductive personality after another" (*ASG*, 68).

Eliot had an eye out for heresy even before his official conversion. His 1926 essay on "Lancelot Andrewes" fixes Andrewes as the model of Christian orthodoxy at the expense of his seventeenth-century contemporary, John Donne. Eliot's comparison of these two spiritual forebears sheds additional light on the divided nature of his critical consciousness. Andrewes earns Eliot's admiration, above all, for the brillance of his intellect. Along with Richard Hooker, Andrewes made the English Church "more worthy of intellectual assent" (*SE*, 301). Reading Andrewes on a theme such as the Incarnation "is like listening to a great Hellenist expounding a test of the *Posterior Analytics*" (*SE*, 304). He speaks not merely from the intellectual power of an individual mind, however, but from the tradition and doctrine of an established institution: "the voice of Andrewes is the voice of a man who has a formed visible Church behind him, who speaks with the old authority and the new culture" (*SE*, 301). Andrewes had what Eliot always searched for and never quite found: "Intellect and sensibility were in harmony." The Elizabethan bishop of Winchester experienced what Eliot saw as the right kind of passion: passion for order in his religion and in his prose. Andrewes could also express emotion, but—to Eliot's approval—the kind of emotion that never overflowed its object: "Andrewes' emotion is purely contemplative, it is not personal, it is wholly evoked by the object of contemplation, to which it is adequate; his emotions wholly contained in and explained by its [*sic*] object" (*SE*, 309).

As for Donne, in 1921 Eliot praised his "direct sensuous apprehension of thought, or a recreation of thought into feeling" (*SE*, 246); but that no longer sufficed for the critic of 1926, when Eliot questions Donne's motives and suspects him, as he suspects Yeats, of deliberately luring his listeners into a trance-like state through the hypnotic power of his language. Without belittling the intensity of Donne's religious experience, Eliot suggests that "this experience was not perfectly controlled and that he lacked spiritual discipline" (*SE*, 302): "He is a little of the religious spellbinder, the Reverend Billy Sunday of his time, the flesh-creeper, the sorcerer of emotional orgy" (*SE*, 302).

Eliot mistrusts Donne for relinquishing the authorial consciousness in his evocation of religious feeling; but, while he condemns Donne on these grounds, he inadvertently makes him much more interesting than Andrewes. He also betrays his own fear of yielding to the seduction of Donne's style. Donne is dangerous partly in his "cunning knowledge of the weakness of the human heart . . . and in a kind of smiling tolerance among his menaces of damnation." Like Lawrence, Donne comes through as something of the Miltonic Satan, all the more insidious for his position within the Church. The danger lies for those who find in his sermons "an indulgence of their sensibility," or those "capable of a certain wantonness of the spirit." The sexual language that penetrates Eliot's discussion shows the critic himself to be one of those most susceptible to temptation. He assesses Donne's character with a mixture of sympathy and mistrust: "Donne had a genuine taste both for theology and for religious emotion; but he belonged to that class of persons, of which there are always one or two examples in the modern world, who seek refuge in religion from the tumults of a strong emotional temperament which can find no complete satisfaction elsewhere" (*SE*, 309). One could find no better words to describe the sensibility of Eliot himself.

3

The final stage of Eliot's development—the years of the *Four Quartets* and the plays—bring a softening of his critical language, even if no actual retreat from his orthodox stance of the late twenties and early thirties. His style gradually loses much of its dogmatic edge, and he focuses more and more on technical matters in poetry, as though he wishes to avoid the violent confrontations that surfaced in his earlier work. Finally, at a point where he has given up writing poems, the elder statesman of Anglo-American letters can speak with equanimity of those demonic forces of the psyche as though he no longer feared their power. The old antagonists of this psychic drama never do join in harmonious union, but at least the fight has gone out of them, and they seem to agree on a reluctant tolerance for each other.

This new spirit of humility in the face of the mysteries of the poetic process characterizes "The Music of Poetry" (1942), in which Eliot acknowledges that the poet who writes about poetry, "at the back of his mind, if not as his ostensible purpose, is always trying to defend the kind of poetry he is writing, or to formulate the kind that he wants to write" (*OPP*, 17). In an essay that concentrates on questions of versification and musical structure in poetry, he only briefly touches on the phenomenological by pointing out how a poem by William Morris intentionally succeeds in producing "the effect of a dream." Far from condemning this intention (as he might have done ten years earlier), Eliot reminds us that "the meaning of a poem may be something larger than its author's conscious purpose, and something remote from its origins" (*OPP*, 22). Similarly, the essay entitled "What Is a Classic?" (1944) devotes detailed attention to matters of cadence, vocabularly, syntax, and the historical development toward "greater complexity of sentence and periodic structure." In contrast to the demons and sirens of earlier years, the metaphor for poetic process here is agricultural: "one is inclined to say that the eighteenth century had perfected its formal garden, only by restricting the area under cultivation" (*OPP*, 61). After more than half a lifetime of rebelling against Yeats's influence (an influence and a rebellion he would deny), Eliot at fifty-two can identify with the Yeats of middle and old age. Quoting from Yeats's *Last Poems*—"You think it horrible that lust and rage / Should dance attendance upon my old age; / They were not such a plague when I was young: / What else have I to spur me into song?"—Eliot can both disapprove and sympathize: "To what honest man, old enough, can these sentiments be entirely alien? They can be subdued and disciplined by religion, but who can say that they are dead?" (*OPP*, 302).

The two-part study of Milton that Eliot included in *On Poetry and Poets* traces for us the gradual cessation of hostilities between the opposing forces of his critical consciousness, and his movement toward a partial reconciliation with the visionary phantasms of the poetic imagination. The essay "Milton I" (1936) appears eleven years before "Milton II" (1947), and it makes only a preliminary shift from the polemics of the period surrounding Eliot's conversion. Eliot does not raise the banner of orthodoxy here; the only "outside standards" he invokes are those of the western poetic tradition itself. He finds Milton a great poet but a bad influence "against which we still have to struggle" (*OPP*, 157).

Milton subjected the English language to deterioration by writing poetry that sacrifices conceptual and visual clarity for the sake of musical effect: "the syntax is determined by the musical significance, by the auditory imagination, rather than by the attempt to follow actual speech or thought" (*OPP*, 161). The "auditory imagination" stands in here for the forces beyond conscious control that Eliot has grappled with elsewhere: he associates it with Joyce's drawing upon "the resources of phantasmagoria" in *Ulysses* (*OPP*, 162) and with images of excessive growth from obscure origins: "a dislocation takes place, through the hypertrophy of the auditory imagination at the expense of the visual and tactile, so that the inner meaning is separated from the surface, and tends to become something occult" (*OPP*, 162). Despite his condemnation of this practice, Eliot shows his receptivity to the auditory imagination by quoting a passage from *Lycidas* "than which for the single effect of grandeur of sound, there is nothing finer in poetry." Significantly for our topology of Eliot's imagination, this passage takes us downward and inward to the fearful depths of the sea, just as the auditory imagination dives below the surface of language: "Where thou perhaps under the whelming tide / Visit'st the bottom of the monstrous world." These lines may strike at the core of Eliot's poetic identity, but officially he approves only their sound, not their imagery or any occult meaning they might have for him. He sticks to his original judgment that although Milton's work "realizes superbly one important element in poetry, he may still be considered as having done damage to the English language from which it has not wholly recovered" (OPP, 164).

By 1947 Eliot has completely reversed his position on Milton, and he seems quite willing to accept his reliance on the mysterious forces of the auditory imagination. The bile has gone out of Eliot's critical style, and he continually tempers his prose with qualifiers and disclaimers. The author of *After Strange Gods* mentions briefly the debate over Milton's Christian orthodoxy, but he backs away immediately: "On these questions I hold no opinion" (OPP, 169). The author of a doctoral dissertation on *Knowledge and Experience in the Philosophy of F. H. Bradley* now confesses to "an incapacity for the abstruse, and an interest in poetry which is primarily a technical interest" (OPP, 171). Where the 1936 essay took pains to point out the harmful effects of Milton's influence, in 1947 "Milton II" proposes the seventeenth-century poet as "one whom poets to-day might study with profit." Eliot praises as Milton's strengths what he saw eleven years earlier as his limitations. For example, Milton's invention of his own poetic language is "one of the marks of his greatness," where its remoteness from ordinary speech had been a weakness. Eliot has similar admiration for Milton's syntax, which in 1936 he had accused of deliberate complication "into what was a previously simplified and abstract thought" (OPP, 160).

Most important for our understanding of Eliot's mellowing sensibility, he comes to terms with the Miltonic imagery that most directly affected the Romantic poets: "I do not think that we should attempt to *see* very clearly any scene that Milton depicts; it should be accepted as a shifting phantasmagory" (OPP, 178). He no longer complains of the abnormal intensification of the auditory imagination at the expense of clear, sharp, visual images: "Our sense of sight must be blurred, so that our *hearing* may become more acute." He even offers that Milton is at his best in "imagery suggestive of vast size, limitless space, abysmal depth, and light and darkness" (*OPP*, 178).

Style and imagery in Eliot's critical writings (as in his poetry) establish a common ground for abysmal depth, the dreamlike, the demonic and sexual, the hallucinatory and phastasmagoric. Quite apart from their ordinary semantic interconnections, these verbal elements occupy a shared position in the symbolic structure of Eliot's language, like the multiple heads of a single hydra rooted deep in the unconscious. Of course they also share an antagonistic role toward that aspect of consciousness which rages for intellectual order. The revisionary evaluations of poets like Milton and Yeats late in Eliot's life point to the exhaustion of that rage, and a new policy of appeasement toward the "demonic, chthonic powers."

Like the later Milton essay, "The Three Voices of Poetry" (1953) avoids the polemic of earlier stages. Here Eliot treats the details of the poetic process dispassionately, and he even expresses resignation in the face of the intractable material of the unconscious. Most of the essay devotes itself to the craftsman's point of view, in its discussion of the second and third voices: the voice of the poet addressing an audience, and the poet's voice when he attempts to create a dramatic character speaking in verse. A poet faces, for example, the problem of finding words for a variety of dramatic characters who differ in intelligence and temperament.

Eliot the critic enriches his imagery only when describing the first voice—the poet talking to himself, or to nobody at all. In contrast to the violent or sexual language Eliot used in the past, he now borrows a primarily *obstetric* metaphor from Gottfried Benn: the obscure poetic impulse begins as an "inert embryo" or "creative germ," which the poet's conscious efforts eventually transform into language: "He is oppressed by a burden which he must bring to birth in order to obtain relief" (*OPP*, 107). This takes place only after a "long process of gestation" of the poem (*OPP*, 109).

In the mythology of the artistic process that emerges from Eliot's criticism as a whole, the poet's conscious mind has relinquished its role of dragon-slayer and assumed the role of midwife:

> In other words again, he is going to all that trouble, not in order
> to communicate with anyone, but to gain relief from acute dis-
> comfort; and when the words are finally arranged in the right
> order—or in what he comes to accept as the best arrangement he
> can find—he may experience a moment of exhaustion, of appease-
> ment, of absolution, and of something very near annihilation,
> which is in itself indescribable [OPP, 107].

C. K. Stead rightly uses this passage to show how the inner, "impersonal" voice of the poet's soul differs from conscious individ-
ualistic thought.[12] Unlike Stead, however, I have concentrated on
the way the language describing this opposition reflects Eliot's
changing attitude toward the poetic process at successive stages
in his career.

This essay of 1953 conveys a distinct sense of diminished possibilities that helps to explain Eliot's lack of serious poetic endeavor since 1942. Rather than attacking the problem of Good
and Evil or perfecting his divine vision, the poet seen here tries
desperately to rid himself of a troublesome burden. What the
poet comes to accept as the best arrangement he can find must
now make do for an earlier ideal union of language and object.
The poet, like the battle-weary critic in Eliot, has thrown down
his sword and now defines himself in terms of exhaustion, appeasement of the aggressor, and something like annihilation.
Eliot's obsession with the demonic has taken on the accents of
defeat, for he no longer invokes moral resistance as a means of
beating it back: the poet "is haunted by a demon, a demon
against which he feels powerless," and which at best he can only
exorcise. "Let the author, at this point, rest in peace" (OPP,
109). The critic's call to arms ends with a plea for negotiated
settlement, and the poet's cry for psychic unity changes into a
cry for mercy, for this unity has become "the aim / Never here to
be realised."

NOTES

1. William Blake, "The Marriage of Heaven and Hell," in *Complete Writings* (London: Oxford University Press, 1969), p. 155; Coleridge, "Principles of Genial Criticism," in Perkins, *English Romantic Writers*, p. 444.

2. This chapter uses the following abbreviations for works by T. S. Eliot: *SW: The Sacred Wood; SE: Selected Essays; UPUC: The Use of Poetry and the Use of Criticism; ASG: After Strange Gods* (New York: Harcourt, Brace, 1934); *OPP: On Poetry and Poets* (New York: Farrar, Straus & Giroux, 1957).

3. Margolis, *T. S. Eliot's Intellectual Development*, p. 25.

4. Bornstein, *Transformations of Romanticism*, ch. 3, pt. 1.

5. Kristian Smidt, *Poetry and Belief in the Work of T. S. Eliot* (New York: Humanities Press, 1961), p. 17.

6. T. S. Eliot, review of *The Cutting of an Agate*, by William B. Yeats, *Athenaeum*, July 4, 1919.

7. T. S. Eliot, "The Borderline of Prose," *New Statesman*, May 19, 1917.

8. Cf. Stead's analysis in *The New Poetic*, p. 127.

9. Boileau, *L'Art poétique*, 3. 256.

10. Delivered in three parts as the Page-Barbour lectures at the University of Virginia in 1933.

11. Bornstein, *Transformations of Romanticism*, p. 149.

12. Stead, *The New Poetic*, p. 143.

Bibliography

BOOKS

Adams, Hazard, ed. *Critical Theory since Plato*. New York: Harcourt Brace Jovanovich, 1971.

Bachelard, Gaston. *La Poétique de l'espace*. Paris: Presses universitaires de France, 1958.

Baudelaire, Charles. *Oeuvres complètes*. Paris: Pléiade, 1975.

Benamou, Michel. *Wallace Stevens and the Symbolist Imagination*. Princeton: Princeton University Press, 1972.

Bergonzi, Bernard. *T. S. Eliot*. New York: Collier Books, 1972.

Blake, William. *Complete Writings*. London: Oxford University Press, 1969.

Bloom, Harold, ed. *Romanticism and Consciousness: Essays in Criticism*. New York: W. W. Norton, 1970.

———. *Yeats*. London: Oxford University Press, 1970.

Boileau-Despréaux, Nicolas. *L'Art poétique*. Paris: Classiques Larousse, 1933.

Bornstein, George. *Transformations of Romanticism in Yeats, Eliot, and Stevens*. Chicago: University of Chicago Press, 1976.

Burke, Kenneth. *Language as Symbolic Action*. Berkeley: University of California Press, 1966.

Coleridge, Samuel Taylor. *Complete Works*. Edited by W. G. T. Shedd. New York: Harper, 1863.

Culler, Jonathan. *Structuralist Poetics*. Ithaca, N.Y.: Cornell University Press, 1975.

Drew, Elizabeth. *T. S. Eliot: The Design of His Poetry*. New York: Scribner's, 1949.

Durand, Gilbert. *Les Structures anthropologiques de l'imaginaire*. Grenoble: Presses universitaires de France, 1960.

Eliot, T. S. *After Strange Gods*. New York: Harcourt, Brace & Co., 1933.

——. *Collected Poems 1909–1962*. New York: Harcourt, Brace & World, 1970.

——. *Complete Poems and Plays 1909–1950*. New York: Harcourt, Brace & World, 1962.

——. *On Poetry and Poets*. New York: Farrar, Straus & Giroux, 1943.

——. *Poems Written in Early Youth*. New York: Farrar, Straus & Giroux, 1967.

——. *The Sacred Wood*. London: Methuen, 1960.

——. *Selected Essays*. New York: Harcourt, Brace & World, 1960.

——. *The Three Voices of Poetry*. Cambridge: National Book League, 1955.

——. *To Criticize the Critic*. New York: Farrar, Straus & Giroux, 1965.

——. *The Use of Poetry and the Use of Criticism*. London: Faber & Faber, 1933.

——. *The Waste Land: A Facsimile and Transcript of the Original Drafts*. Edited by Valerie Eliot. New York: Harcourt Brace Jovanovich, 1971.

——, trans. *Anabasis*, by Saint-John Perse. London: Faber & Faber, 1959.

Frye, Northrop, ed. *Romanticism Reconsidered*. New York: Columbia University Press, 1963.

Gallup, Donald. *T. S. Eliot: A Bibliography*. New York: Harcourt, Brace & World, 1969.

Gardner, Helen. *The Composition of "Four Quartets."* New York: Oxford University Press, 1978.

Gordon, Lyndall. *T. S. Eliot's Early Years*. Oxford: Oxford University Press, 1977.

Heidegger, Martin. *Being and Time*. Translated by John Macquarrie and Edward Robinson. New York: Harper & Row, 1962.

Hume, Robert Ernest, trans. *The Thirteen Principal Upanishads*. London: Oxford University Press, 1949.

Kenner, Hugh. *The Invisible Poet: T. S. Eliot*. New York: Obolensky, 1959.

Kierkegaard, Søren. *The Concept of Dread*. Translated by Walter Lowrie. Princeton: Princeton University Press, 1944.

Kuhn, Helmut. *Encounter with Nothingness: An Essay on Existentialism*. London: Methuen, 1951.

Langbaum, Robert. *The Poetry of Experience: The Dramatic Mono-*

logue in Modern Literary Tradition. London: Chatto & Windus, 1957.

Lynch, William F., S.J. *Christ and Apollo: The Dimensions of the Literary Imagination*. New York: Sheed & Ward, 1960.

Mallarmé, Stéphane. *Oeuvres complètes*. Paris: Pléiade, 1974.

Margolis, John D. *T. S. Eliot's Intellectual Development*. Chicago: University of Chicago Press, 1972.

Martin, Jay, ed. *A Collection of Critical Essays on "The Waste Land."* Englewood Cliffs, N.J.: Prentice-Hall, 1968.

Matthiessen, F. O. *The Achievement of T. S. Eliot*. London: Sheed & Ward, 1948.

Maxwell, D. E. S. *The Poetry of T. S. Eliot*. London: Oxford University Press, 1958.

Melville, Herman. *Moby-Dick*. With an introduction by Harold Beaver. Harmondsworth, England: Penguin Books, 1972.

Moody, A. D. *Thomas Stearns Eliot: Poet*. Cambridge: At the University Press, 1979.

Nerval, Gerard de. *Les Chimères*. Paris: Garnier-Flammarion, 1965.

Perkins, David, ed. *English Romantic Writers*. New York: Harcourt, Brace & World, 1967.

Rajan, Balachandra, ed. *T. S. Eliot: A Study of His Writings by Several Hands*. London: Dobson, 1947.

Rees, Thomas R. *The Technique of T. S. Eliot*. The Hague: Mouton, 1974.

Rosenthal, M. L. *The Modern Poets*. London: Oxford University Press, 1960.

Schneider, Elisabeth. *T. S. Eliot: The Pattern in the Carpet*. Berkeley: University of California Press, 1975.

Smidt, Kristian. *Poetry and Belief in the Work of T. S. Eliot*. New York: Humanities Press, 1961.

Smith, Grover. *T. S. Eliot's Poetry and Plays*. Chicago: University of Chicago Press, 1950.

Southam, B. C. *A Guide to the Selected Poems of T. S. Eliot*. New York: Harcourt, Brace & World, 1968.

Spender, Stephen. *T. S. Eliot*. Harmondsworth, England: Penguin Books, 1975.

St. John of the Cross. *The Dark Night of the Soul*. Translated and edited by Kurt F. Reinhardt. New York: Ungar, 1957.

Stead, C. K. *The New Poetic: Yeats to Eliot*. London: Hutchinson University Library, 1964.

Tate, Allen, ed. *T. S. Eliot: The Man and His Work*. New York: Delta, 1966.

Traversi, Derek. *T. S. Eliot: The Longer Poems*. New York: Harcourt Brace Jovanovich, 1976.

Williamson, George. *A Reader's Guide to T. S. Eliot*. 2d ed. New York: Farrar, Straus & Giroux, 1966.

Yeats, William Butler. *Collected Poems*. New York: Macmillan, 1956.

ARTICLES

Abrams, M. H. "Structure and Style in the Greater Romantic Lyric." In *Romanticism and Consciousness*, edited by Harold Bloom, pp. 201–29. New York: Norton, 1970.

Bille, Finn. "The Ultimate Metaphor and the Defeat of Poetry in T. S. Eliot's *Four Quartets*." *International Journal of Symbology* 3 (1972):16–24.

Brooks, Cleanth. *"The Waste Land*: Critique of the Myth." In *A Collection of Critical Essays on "The Waste Land*," edited by Jay Martin. Englewood Cliffs, N. J.: Prentice-Hall, 1968.

Brooks, Harold F. "Between *The Waste Land* and the First Ariel Poems: 'The Hollow Men.' " *English* 16 (1966):89:93.

Eliot, T. S. "Beyle and Balzac." *Athenaeum*, May 30, 1919, pp. 392–93.

———. "The Borderline of Prose." *New Statesman*, May 19, 1917, pp. 157–59.

———. "Deux Attitudes Mystiques: Dante et Donne." *Chroniques* 3 (1927):149–73 (Roseau d'Or, no. 14).

[———]. "Mr. Yeats' Swan Song." *Athenaeum*, April 4, 1919, pp. 136–37.

———. "Note sur Mallarmé et Poe." *Nouvelle revue française* 14 (1926):524–26.

Garber, Frederick. "Nature and the Romantic Mind: Egotism, Empathy, Irony." *Comparative Literature* 29 (1977):193–212.

Gardner, Helen. *"Four Quartets*: A Commentary." In *T. S. Eliot: A Study of His Writing by Several Hands*, edited by Balachandra Rajan. London: Dobson, 1947.

Harmon, William. "T. S. Eliot's Raids on the Inarticulate." *PMLA* 91 (1976):450–59.

Hough, Graham. "Vision and Doctrine in *Four Quartets*." *Critical Quarterly* 15:107–27.

Poulet, Georges. "Phenomenology of Reading." Translated by Elliott Coleman. In *Critical Theory since Plato*, edited by Hazard Adams, pp. 1213–23. New York: Harcourt Brace Jovanovich, 1971.

Spanos, William V. " 'Wanna Go Home, Baby?': *Sweeney Agonistes* as Drama of the Absurd." *PMLA* 85:8–20.

Wimsatt, William K., Jr. "The Structure of Romantic Nature Imagery." In *Romanticism and Consciousness*, edited by Harold Bloom, pp. 77–88. New York: Norton, 1970.

Index

About the Author

DAVID SPURR was born in Princeton, New Jersey. He attended the University of Michigan, where he received his Ph.D. in comparative literature in 1978. From 1971 to 1973 he worked as a staff correspondent for United Press International in France and in Eastern Europe. His publications include articles on modern and comparative literature as well as journalistic pieces on a variety of subjects. He is currently assistant professor of English at the University of Illinois at Chicago.